What does it take
to become a sales success?

Why are you not succeeding at sales
to the best of your ability?

Why do you believe that other things,
other people, or your boss
are holding you back?

Why do you lose sales to competition
just because they cut their price?

Why do your customers
not reorder from you?

Why do you believe you're underpaid?

Why are you not earning
the money you feel you deserve?

**Because you don't have
all the answers...yet!**

**This book contains the answers.
99.5 Real World Answers That Make Sense,
Make Sales, and Make Money.**

Jeffrey Gitomer's

LITTLE RED BOOK
of SALES ANSWERS

99.5 Real World Answers
That Make Sense,
Make Sales, and Make Money

Prentice Hall

The Little Red Book of Sales Answers

PEARSON

Prentice
Hall

Published by Prentice Hall, Upper Saddle River, New Jersey 07458.
Vice President and Editor-in-Chief: Tim Moore.

To order additional copies of this title, contact your local bookstore
or call 704.333.1112.
The author may be contacted at the following address:
BuyGitomer
310 Arlington Ave., Loft 329
Charlotte, NC 28203
Phone 704.333.1112, fax 704.333.1011
E-mail: salesman@gitomer.com
Web sites: www.gitomer.com, www.trainone.com

Cover Design by Josh Gitomer.
Photography by Mitchell Kearney.
Page design by Greg Russell.
Edited by Jessica McDougall and Rachel Russotto.

Printed in China by R.R. Donnelley.

Box set edition, October 2007

Library of Congress Cataloging-in-Publication Data

Gitomer, Jeffrey H.
  Jeffrey Gitomer's little red book of sales answers.
      p. cm.
  ISBN 0-13-173536-5 (hardcover : alk. paper)
  ISBN 978-0-13-173536-1
  1. Selling. 2. Business networks. 3. Customer loyalty. 4. Customer
relations. I. Title: Little red book of sales answers. II. Title.
  HF5438.25.G578 2006
  658.85--dc22

                                        2005030574

74% of all salespeople don't know the *BEST* answers to their selling situations, opportunities, and barriers.

They don't always have the *BEST* answers about where they are, what to say, what to do, or how to do it…in a way that results in a sale!

Every major sales answer you need to know is in this book.

Salespeople are looking for answers.

The fastest, easiest answers that work every time.

The good news is, the answers exist. The bad news is, in order to be able to become a successful salesperson, you have to understand, practice, and master the answers.

You'd think with all the answers contained in this book, that anyone who reads it would automatically become a better salesperson. You'd be thinking wrong.

To become a better salesperson, the first thing you have to do is **read it**. The second thing to do with this book is **read it again**. The third thing to do with this book is **try one answer everyday**. If it doesn't work exactly right the first time, or the outcome wasn't what you expected, try it again and tweak it a little bit. The fourth thing you have to do is **practice the answer** until you feel that it's working. The fifth thing you have to do is **become the master of it**.

SECRET: Blend each answer to your selling situation and do it in a way that fits your style, and your personality.

Think about the way you ask for an appointment. The way you leave a voice-mail message. The way you follow up after a sales call. The way you begin a sales presentation. The way you ask for a sale. The way you respond to an angry customer. The way you earn a referral. Or the way you get a testimonial. Wouldn't you love to have the perfect answer for every one of these situations?

You're in luck, Sparky! Those and 99.5 other answers are contained in this book. Real world answers, for real world selling situations. Answers that you can use the minute you read them -- and then take the results to the bank -- your bank.

My brother, Josh, proclaims that there are no answers – only questions. Fortunately, my brother is a choral director and a graphic designer, not a salesperson. He is partially right in that many of these questions will beget deeper questions. Those are the ones that you'll have to answer yourself. Those are the ones that you'll be able to easily figure out because of the other 99.5 answers contained in this book.

The most important thing to understand is that you are the master of your own fate. And a large portion of that hinges on how you master these answers. How you use these answers can control the outcome of your sales.

GREAT NEWS! Your sales job is actually *your own business* within your company's business. The sales you make cause the orders to be entered on the books, start the machinery, ship the products, and generate the invoices that ultimately result in cash from customers. That cash pays you and everybody else in the company, including the CEO and the owner.

In 1946 the late, great Red Motley said, "Nothing happens until a sale is made." Sixty years later -- those words are more meaningful than ever. Your job is to make the sale. By reading this book, and mastering its answers, you'll be able to go out and make the sale -- before your competition does.

THE WEIGHT OF THE SALES WORLD IS ON YOUR SHOULDERS.

Throughout this book, you'll see

SALES ATLAS

at the top of the page.

He's holding up the page titles the same way you have to hold up your company -- the weight of your company's sales success rests on your shoulders. You carry the weight of the sales world.

Here's the good news: When you make all the sales that your company's hoping you make, you'll be in perfect shape -- perfect *physical* shape -- to carry all your money to the bank!

What's the best way to make a sale?

The BEST way to make a sale is to become friendly before you start.

The BEST way to make a sale is to find some common ground before you begin the selling process.

The BEST way to make a sale is to ask intelligent questions that draw out both needs and motives.

The BEST way to make a sale is to relax throughout the sales conversation.

The BEST way to make a sale is to ask for a date of beginning, or some type of commitment to move forward after you are certain you have removed all the risks, and all the barriers, from your prospect's ying process.

The BEST way to make a sale is to create an atmosphere where the other guy wants to buy.

FINAL ANSWER: The reality is -- there's no "one best way." But these "best" elements, when combined, will kick your competition into the dirt. (Where they belong!)

THE LITTLE RED BOOK of SALES ANSWERS

99.5 Real World Answers That Make Sense,
Make Sales, and Make Money

Table of Contents

PART ONE ....p. 2-30
Personal Improvement That Leads to Personal Growth

PART TWO ....p. 31-55
Prospecting for Golden Leads and Making Solid Appointments

PART THREE ....p. 56-74
How to Win the Sales Battle AND the Sales War

PART FOUR ....p. 75-142
Sales Skill Building...One Brick at a Time

PART FIVE ....p. 143-178
Building the Friendship. Building the Relationship. Earning the
Referral. Earning the Testimonial. Earning the Reorder.

PART SIX ....p. 179-192
Building Your Personal Brand

PART SIX point FIVE ....p. 193-197
The Final AHA!

What do you want to know?

PART ONE
Personal Improvement That Leads to Personal Growth

1. What is the meaning of sales?
2. How do I become the successful person I dream about, and deserve to be?
3. How do I do my best every day?
4. How do I attain, achieve, and maintain a positive attitude?
5. How can I improve my humor?
6. How can I improve my creativity?
7. How can I improve my writing skills?
8. My company won't buy me a laptop. What should I do?
9. How do I get a mentor, and how do I build a relationship once I find one?
10. What causes my fear of failure, and how do I get over dejection caused by rejection?
11. What is the secret of worry-free living?
12. What books should be in my library? What are the best tapes and CDs to listen to in the car?
13. Should I change jobs?
14. Should I sign a non-compete?

PART TWO
Prospecting for Golden Leads and Making Solid Appointments

15. How do I make a cold call?
16. How can I STOP making cold calls and still make appointments?
17. How can I get around a lower-level person?
18. What is the best way to get information to a prospect?
19. What is the best way to get past the gatekeeper?

20. What is the best way to get information on a prospect before a sales appointment?

21. What is the best way to set an appointment?

22. How do I find out who the real decision maker is?

23. What do I do when the prospect doesn't show for an appointment?

24. What do I do when the prospect lies?

25. What questions am I asking my prospects and customers that my competition isn't asking?

26. Why did the last five prospects say no? What am I doing about it?

27. Why did the last 10 prospects say yes? How am I building on that?

PART THREE

How to Win the Sales Battle AND the Sales War

28. What is the best way to approach a sale?

29. What are the two most killer questions in sales?

30. What are the three dumbest questions in sales?

31. What is the best way to control a phone conversation?

32. How do I get around the price objection? (Who brought up price anyway?)

33. What is the difference between a stall and an objection?

34. How can I prevent objections from occurring?

35. How do I recognize buying signals? What is the most powerful buying signal?

36. What is the best time and way to ask for the sale?

37. How do buyers decide, and what are buyers looking for?

PART FOUR
Sales Skill Building -- One Brick at a Time

38. Why do buyers not return my call? How do I get my calls returned?

39. What does the voice-mail message I leave say to my customers?

40. What is the best way to use the Internet to make sales?

41. Should I try to "type" the buyer?

42. What is the best way to prepare for a sales call?

43. Should I honor a "No Soliciting" sign?

44. What is the best way to beat the competition?

45. What is the best way to ensure I get a reorder?

46. What is the best way to follow up?

47. What are the best ways to add value?

48. What is "give value first?"

49. How can I create more valuable questions?

50. What is the "sale after the sale?"

51. Why do customers cancel?

52. What is the best way to get out of a slump?

53. What are the biggest mistakes salespeople make?

54. What are the fatal flaws of selling?

55. What should a business lunch consist of?

56. Should I golf for business? How?

57. What should I say when the customer calls and he's mad as hell?

58. How can I prevent the prospect from going with the lowest price?

59. How can I make my proposal stand out?

60. What is the best way to use testimonials?

61. What do I say to my customer when my competition lies about me, my product, or my company?

62. How do I beat "Call Reluctance?"

63. What kind of thank you note should I write?
64. How excellent are my selling skills?
65. What is the best way to make my quota every month?
66. What is the best way to manage my time?
67. Why do I quit so easy when the customer tells me, "No?" How long should I have hung in there?
68. What is the best way to double my sales this year?
69. Who is the most important person in the world?
70. How much time should I invest in promoting and positioning my business?
71. How am I helping my customers build their business?
72. What am I doing to earn my customers loyalty?
73. How vulnerable am I to our competition?
74. What do I need to learn to get ahead? What do I have to do to get ahead?

PART FIVE

Building the Friendship. Building the Relationship. Earning the Referral. Earning the Testimonial. Earning the Reorder.

75. How easy is it to do business with me?
76. How friendly are the employees at my company? How friendly is my boss? How friendly am I?
77. How can I establish rapport?
78. What is the best way to begin a relationship?
79. Where should I network?
80. How do I develop a powerful 30-second commercial?
81. How much time should I devote to networking?
82. What are the secrets of networking success?
83. How do I get better leads than anyone else?
84. How do I get testimonials?
85. How powerful is a testimonial in completing a sale?
86. What am I doing to prevent the loss of my best customers?

87. Am I available to my customers when they need me?

88. What value am I bringing to my customer beyond my product and service?

89. Why will some customers leave?

90. How do I get more referrals?

91. What is the best way to approach and work a referral?

92. How many people are spreading my "word" for me?

PART SIX
Building Your Personal Brand

93. How can I differentiate myself from the competition?

94. How often am I in front of my customers?

95. What can I do to my Web site to entice my customers to buy from me?

96. What am I "known" for?

97. Are you a sales leader or a sales chaser?

98. What am I recognized as being the "THE BEST" at?

99. What do the leaders in my industry say about me?

PART SIX point FIVE
The Final AHA!

99.5 How much do I love what I do?

THAT'S A HELL OF A LOT OF QUESTIONS!

QUIT YOUR WHINING. ALL OF THE ANSWERS ARE INSIDE.

"I wish I would have said…"

Ever said that? Sure you have. Everybody has. You said it early in life, and after tests you took in school. You said it after communicating with friends, siblings, and parents. You said it all throughout your growing up years, and into adulthood.

Now it's game time. Sales time. "I wish I would have said…" has no place in the world of sales, other than in the mouths of sales losers.

The second best answer
in sales is first loser.

The second best answer
in sales can cost you a million dollars.

The second best answer
in sales can cost you your customer.

The second best answer
in sales can cost you your job.

If you want the best answers to the most important questions of selling (and of life), you've come to the right book.

All you have to do now is learn them better than your competitor.

99.5
Real World
Answers

Answers you can take out
into the street the minute you read
them and turn them into money!

PART ONE

Personal Improvement That Leads to Personal Growth

WHAT ARE THE BEST ANSWERS?

HOW SHOULD I KNOW? I HAVEN'T READ THE BOOK YET.

I KNOW ALL THE ANSWERS, EXCEPT ONE. HOW AM I GOING TO MAKE MY CAR PAYMENT THIS MONTH?

What is the meaning of sales?

Every salesperson (you included) wants to know the fastest, easiest, bestest way to make a sale.

One day I asked an audience of insurance salespeople, "How many of you would like it if I gave you a list of people who wanted to buy insurance now?" Everyone raised their hand.

HINT: There is no list. But every salesperson wishes that one would be handed to them.

The one-word meaning of sales is: **WORK**

The two-word meaning of sales is: **WORK HARD**

No surprise there -- unless of course you're working at Disney World, over there in Fantasyland. Wake up, Tinkerbell. There's no magic wand. There's no secret formula. There's no lotion or potion that will make sales faster and easier for you -- unless your potion is hard work.

Oh sure, you'll get lucky every once in a while, and think that it had something to do with your skill. But how many people do you know that were in the right place, at the right time, and got the biggest sale of their lives just by being there? You wrote it off to luck. I don't.

The reason they made the "lucky" sale is that they were in the right place, at the right time, and they were prepared. So let's add another word to this formula. **Prepare**.

Well, if you're prepared, and you work hard, then you should be ready to make the sale, right? Wrong. Next you have to engage. **Engage** in a way that the customer will come to buy.

So if you work hard, prepare, and engage you should make the sale, right? Wrong. You have to **get a commitment** from the probable purchaser that he or she is willing to buy what you have to sell.

If you make a sale and just run away, you won't make a fortune -- you'll make a commission. The key is to work hard, prepare, engage, get a commitment, earn a sale, earn a reorder, earn a referral, and earn a testimonial. Then (and only then) you can build on the sale, build success, and build wealth.

Take a look at the formula that I've given you, and come to the realization that if there's any magic to it, *you* are the magician.

There remains one more critical part in the formula. And as the magician you certainly know the secret. If you ask any magician how he or she became incredibly proficient at performing their magic, they will all answer with one word: **Practice**. There you have it, Houdini. Now go pull a sale out of your hat.

How do I become the successful person I dream about, and deserve to be?

ANSWER: Set achievable goals.

Where will I be one year from today?

Where will my sales be?

How will I get there?

Are my real-world goals established?

Are they written down?
(If not, next year you'll likely
be where you are today.)

You know the classic definition of a goal:
A dream -- with a plan and a deadline.

The classic 3.5 reasons people (you included) don't achieve their goals are:

1. Failure to write your goals down and post them in plain view.

2. Failure to make a plan to achieve the goals.

3. Failure to commit, or live up to the commitments they made.

3.5 Failure to make goals that were achievable in the first place.

These seem pretty easy to overcome, but studies show that more than 74% of our adult society doesn't even put their goals in writing. WOW!

Here are 7.5 classic steps to goal setting and achievement:

1. Identify it. Write your goal(s) down clearly. Write exactly what you want to achieve…in the most specific terms possible.

2. Date it. Put a date (and a time limit) to start the goal, and finish it. Unless you commit to a start and target an end, your ability to achieve any goal is questionable.

3. List the obstacles you will have to overcome to achieve your goal. Identification of obstacles will help prevent them from occurring.

4. List the groups and people to contact who will work with you and help you achieve your goal. People will help you if you ask.

5. Make a list of the skills and knowledge you need to have to achieve your goal. Do you have them, or do you need to acquire them? Make a plan to acquire or hire the knowledge or skills you need.

6. Make (and write down) an action plan for each goal. The more specific and detailed your plan is, the more likely you are to enact it.

7. List the benefits of goal achievement. What's in it for me after I achieve this goal? What's my incentive? Is my incentive strong enough to ensure achievement?

7.5 Take action every day. It only takes ten or fifteen minutes a day to chip away at goal achievement. Make a personal commitment to act on your goals…and live up to that commitment every day.

Goal achievement is up to you. Your self-talk, self-visualization, and self-determination are 90% of the achievement process.

The big secret of goal achievement is to figure out "the daily dose."

Determine how much you need to do each day to reach your goal in short steps. An amount you can measure. An amount you can achieve.

Save pennies per day, lose ounces per day, make calls per day, earn dollars per sale -- and achieve that daily dose each day.

Finally, you achieve the goal.
At last you can say the magic words.

Scream them -- I DID IT!
(Screaming positive things always feels wonderful.)

Free Red✗**Bit:** Want the Gitomer CliffsNotes to new classic goal achievement? Go to www.gitomer.com, register if you are a first time user, and enter the word CLIFFSNOTES in the RedBit box.

How do I do my best every day?

Here are a few simple rules:

1. Wake up early. The early bird does not get the worm. The early bird makes the money. Work while others sleep.

2. Love what you do. If you don't love it, you will never rise to the top. Love it, or leave it.

3. Dedicate yourself to being a life-long student. How many books did you read last year?

4. Convert anger to resolve. Anger is the biggest waste of energy on the planet. It blocks positive thought. It blocks creative thought.

5. Convert barrier to breakthrough. You may know it as objection. Or even rejection. Stick at it until you win, and you will gain personal, mental dominance.

6. Take every "no" as "not yet." You don't hear with your ears. You hear with your mind. The way you accept other's words will determine your fate. Gain an attitude of positive acceptance.

7. Watch little or no television. You'll never succeed watching television. Convert TV time to study time. Convert TV time to preparation time. Convert TV time to thinking time. **Invest your time, don't spend it.**

8. Read for twenty minutes every morning. Reading provides the opportunity for quiet insight. You can reflect on the ideas and thoughts of others, and immediately convert them to your own success formula. Your best chance for success is reading. Learn to earn. Read to succeed.

9. Write for twenty minutes every morning. What should you write about? Anything you want! Begin to clarify your thoughts and ideas in writing.

10. Call people you love -- and tell them you love them. Love is not motivation. Love is inspiration. To be your best, you must go beyond motivation -- to inspiration.

10.5 Tell yourself you're the best. "I am the greatest of all time." Muhammad Ali said that thousands of times. Millions of people agree he was the greatest of all time. He began that journey by telling himself first. So can you.

TAKE OUT THE TRASH.
CHANGE THE LITTER.
STOP AT THE DRUG STORE.
PICK UP THE DRY CLEANING.
MOW THE LAWN.

SOME DAYS IT'S HARD
TO BE YOUR BEST.

How do I attain, achieve, and maintain a positive attitude?

Most everyone thinks they have a positive attitude, but they don't. Usually not even close. They don't understand the essence of "attitude." It's not a feeling -- it's a state of mind that is self-induced. You are in complete control of it. You determine what your attitude is.

It has nothing to do with what happens to you.
It's not about money or success. It is, pure and simple,
the way you dedicate yourself to the way you think.

Here's the lifetime formula to attaining a positive attitude:

1. Surround yourself with positive things and positive people.

2. Read and listen to positive books, CDs, and tapes.

3. Say all things in a positive way. How you *can*, not why you *can't*.

4. Believe you can achieve it.

5. Don't listen to others who tell you you're nuts. They're just jealous.

5.5 Start now and work at it every day. Simple? Yes. But it takes hard work.

To achieve a positive attitude you must study it, and practice the self-discipline of it. You must live the essence of it -- every day.

My secret for sustaining it? I read two pages from a positive book every morning -- Napoleon Hill, Dale Carnegie, Norman Vincent Peale. And I have listened to the Earl Nightingale recording of *The Strangest Secret* once a month (or more) for the past 30 years.

Want to start from the beginning? Re-read *The Little Engine That Could*. It's not a book for a kid. It's a philosophy for a lifetime.

Attitude is something you give yourself over time. Day by day. And others can catch it from you. Or not. There is no "Instant Positive Attitude" – only "Instant Negative Attitude."

You have a choice!

Positive attitude is a self-imposed blessing. And it is my greatest hope that you discover that truth and bless yourself forever.

How can I improve my humor?

You can start by studying humor. There are all kinds of books available on the subject. Pick one that suits your style. Then go to humorous events at comedy clubs and watch laughable movies. Set the stage for beginning your study and understanding of humor.

SECRET: Don't just go to laugh, go to learn. Don't just watch, take notes and learn.

ANOTHER SECRET: Humor is a "sense." You often say that someone has a great "sense of humor." To get funnier, to get more humorous, you have to sense when the humor occurs. Be more alert, so that you'll know (sense) when to make humor yourself.

Hang around funny people. What makes them funny? Isn't it usually a combination of who they are, what they say, and their style of delivery? Don't copy them. Just look at their qualities and adapt them to your style. Be comfortable with your humor. Make it your own.

CAUTION: Don't make humor at other people's expense. If you want to make a joke about somebody, make it about yourself. And don't retell jokes. If the other person's heard it, you look like a fool. Especially if you're not a good joke teller.

When something funny happens, how do you react? Do you laugh, or do you sneer? The way you react to funny will often determine how funny you're capable of being. I know people that think nothing is funny. I don't know them well, because I try to avoid them.

FINAL ANSWER: The easiest way to improve your humor is to "think funny" first. Note: I did not say "corny." I said "funny." If you have humor at the top of your mind -- it'll become a habit that leads to smiles, and those smiles are contagious. It's all in the way you look at things.

Your challenge is to embrace funny as part of your everyday life.

How can I improve my creativity?

There are two authors who have provided a foundation for my creative study: Edward de Bono and Michael Michalko. Start with Michalko's *Thinkertoys*: the easiest and most practical book on creativity ever written. Then progress to de Bono's *Six Thinking Hats*.

HERE'S THE SECRET: Read slowly. A page or two a day. Maybe one chapter per week. And as you read a concept or strategy or technique -- try it out. Try it out everyday. This will give you a depth of understanding in your own real world. Book learning is useless without practical application.

Select five areas of your sales skills (or life skills) in which you would like to be more creative. Maybe it's a cold call, or your voice mail, or follow-up, or how to say thank you. Maybe it's a birthday present for your kid. Apply the lessons you've learned (from studying) to these situations by trying different ideas -- no matter how silly they may seem.

They start out silly -- they end up smart.

Ask the guy trying to invent an x-ray machine that ended up being television. Seemed silly at the time.

Here's what I do: Almost all of my customers have children or grandchildren. Instead of buying a traditional bottle of wine or booze, or giving them some silly corporate trinket, I give them children's books. Books that have won awards and that have been signed by the author. For less than thirty dollars, I've made the most memorable impression possible on a human being.

I got this idea by applying the principles of Michael Michalko's creative concept called SCAMPER.

Now it's your turn.

Free Red Bit: What is SCAMPER? Go to www.gitomer.com, register if you are a first time user, and enter the word SCAMPER in the RedBit box.

How can I improve my writing skills?

I learned how to write from my dad and my brother.

Here are a few GUIDELINES to improve your writing skills:

- Improve your writing by reading good writers.
- Improve your writing by practicing every day.
- Improve your writing by editing a day later.
- Improve your writing by establishing a structure.
- Improve your writing by finding your "voice."
- Improve your writing by understanding that factual, listed content is powerful.
- Adverbs, prepositional phrases, and "est" are out.
- Use the right tone. Mine is straight forward, succinct.
- Select a "voice of author." Mine is authoritative.
- Use the power of authority in pronouns: first person singular, second person, third person.
- Use writer's privilege: writing in vernacular, not grammar. Use incorrect syntax like "ain't" and "gonna" for emphasis.
- Grammar (OK sometimes). For me, it's write like you speak.
- Research vs. your knowledge. Proof vs. opinion. I use knowledge and opinion.
- Use graphic and alliterative word choices like "vomit" and "puke."

- Keep paragraphs short.
- Use repeated themes. I use: MAJOR CLUE, or "Think about this..."
- Use **bold** and CAPS to make points, and emphasize words.
- Grab me at the beginning. Start with a question or short statement.
- Give me meat in the middle. All meat.
- Make me smile, think, or act at the end. End with impact.

BIG SECRET: Read aloud when you edit. How does it *sound*, not how does it read.

ASK YOURSELF THIS: Where's the impact? Where's the meat? Where's the point? Where's the hook? Is it compelling? Will the reader want to read it all? Will the reader *think* as a result of this writing? Will the reader *act* as a result of this writing?

MAJOR CLUE: When is the last time you wrote an article in a publication that your customers and prospects read? The answer to that question is most likely, "never." Wouldn't it be cool if you walked in on a sales call and saw the magazine you wrote in -- open to the page where your article appears -- on the desk of your probable purchaser?

Writing is a key differentiator. I've used it for 14 years. Writing will not just lead to differentiation. Writing is the credibility you need to create buyer confidence.

8

My company won't buy me a laptop. What should I do?

Go out and invest it in the most important person in the world -- YOU!

The worst part about this scenario is that you'll whine to other people, and you'll whine to your boss. Maybe you'll even whine to your customers. In other words, you're a whiner. Eventually, you'll quit your job only to go whine someplace else, because you quit for a symptom, not a problem.

In your mind, you quit because they wouldn't buy you a laptop. The reality is, you weren't willing to invest in yourself. And the same will hold true in your next job.

The worst thing that can happen is at your next job they *do* buy you a laptop, and you don't learn the lesson.

ANSWER: Your success is your responsibility. So are your sales tools. Go down to the computer store and buy one yourself. You have your own money now. *Go out and invest it in the most important person in the world -- YOU!*

This holds true for anything your company won't supply you with. Suppose they won't pay for your gasoline. Are you gonna leave your car on the side of the road? How about food? You gonna stop eating?

How about stop whining, and start winning?

How do I get a mentor, and how do I build the relationship once I find one?

Approach potential mentors with care and respect. Go slow. You find mentors by earning their respect -- *not* by asking them to be your mentor. They just become one over time.

SUCCESS CHALLENGE: Make a short list of people (possible mentors) you believe can impact your career. Find a way to get to know them. Find a way to get them to know you. Find a way to get the impact of *their* success, to have an impact on *your* success.

Here's a list of guidelines that will grow a mentoring relationship:

☛ **Use your mentor wisely.** Don't over use or abuse your privilege.

☛ **Don't ask your mentor for money.** It will prejudice their response, and you will lose their objectivity.

☛ **Your mentor takes pride in your growth.** Your mentor enjoys helping you -- BUT -- you must thank and acknowledge them at every opportunity. Show them you did what they suggested and it worked. That's their inspiration to continue.

You keep a mentor for years and years by bringing value to the relationship. Share your goals. Ask for their advice, their opinion, their experience. Share your triumphs. Ask to hear about theirs. Share your defeats, don't moan about them. Tell them what has happened, and ask for advice. Tell them what you intend to do -- then do it.

PERSONAL NOTE: Mentor's wisdom has played a major role in my growth and success. I had five mentors, including my dad. Three are still alive. Their wisdom has been a guiding light, spiritual lift, wake-up call, and cold slap in the face when I needed it most.

Sometimes it hurts to hear the right answer. Sometimes it's a relief.

I owe more to my mentors than can be expressed in writing. They know it, too. I've told them. More important -- I've shown them -- by adopting their wisdom, adopting their philosophies, and putting their advice into action.

Find mentors at the top! If you're seeking help, get it from those who have been through the battle -- and won.

Mentors can help you with the value of their experience, with the wisdom gained from their success and failure, with practical advice that often flies in the face of the emotional frenzy of the present moment, and with ideas and concepts that go beyond your present vision.

Free Red✗Bit: Want to learn more about why mentors are valuable? Go to www.gitomer.com, register if you are a first time user, and enter the words MENTOR VALUE in the RedBit box.

What causes my fear of failure, and how do I get over dejection caused by rejection?

Fear of failure or fear of rejection, like any other fear, is predominantly mental. But it may be mental based on your past experiences. You may have failed in the past. You may have been rejected a lot in the past. You may have been in a tough family or personal situation and lost some of the feeling of pride or self-worth that you once had. You may be "expecting" to lose.

Substitute your negative sense for your positive sense. Here are the negative senses and the positive substitutes:

NEGATIVES:

1. The sense of fear.
2. The sense of nervousness.
3. The sense of rejection.
4. The sense of procrastination or reluctance.
5. The sense of justification/rationale.
6. The sense of self-doubt.
7. The sense of uncertainty.
8. The sense of doom.
8.5 The sense of "I'm unlucky."

POSITIVES:

1. The sense of confidence.
2. The sense of positive anticipation.
3. The sense of determination.
4. The sense of achievement.
5. The sense of winning.
6. The sense of success.
7. The sense of "I'm certain."
8. The sense of "sunny day."

8.5 The sense of good fortune.

FINAL ANSWER: In any given situation, where the chance is win or lose, succeed or not succeed, be accepted or be rejected, you must be able to recall every past success that you've ever had and dwell on that. Dwell on the fact that you *can* be a winner -- because you *have* been a winner.

What is the secret of worry-free living?

Want a few answers? No problem, I've got them. And they all stem from the philosophy of one (MAD) man. Read on…

Sweat. Jog. Work out. Shower. Physical exercise, followed by relaxation, will clear your mind. Positive ideas and innovative thoughts will just pop in. I promise.

Relax. Walk. A two-block walk clears the head, and solutions will follow. Watch a funny, old movie (W.C. Fields, Marx Brothers) or a funny TV rerun (*Honeymooners*). Veg out for an hour. Clear your mind with fresh air and fresh humor.

Identify. Worry is a symptom, not a problem. Source the cause. Before you can get rid of worry, you must identify its real cause. The real cause of your worry may surprise you.

Plan. Once you identify the area that causes worry, change it into an *action plan for success*. Write a separate plan for each item. Create ways to look at it differently. Adopt a better attitude toward it. Or just avoid it. Don't be afraid or embarrassed to enlist the aid of others. They may be glad to help you (and help themselves at the same time).

Read. Reading gives you a mental rest or mental boost. Reading forces you to turn off the television. The best book on the subject of stress and worry was written 50 years ago.

Dale Carnegie wrote *How to Stop Worrying and Start Living*. Have you read it? Buy it. Read it.

Act. Don't act *on* the worry, act *against* it. Create a positive reaction to the worry. I've had a statue on my bookshelf since 1959. It's a ceramic bust of *MAD* magazine's Alfred E. Newman. Inscribed on the statue is his famous (only) quote, "What -- me worry?" It's been my credo for more years than I care to acknowledge, but it's also one of the deep dark secrets of sales success (or causes of sales failure).

Smile. It's contagious. It sets a good mood both externally and internally. In sales, it's a prerequisite. If you do it all the time, every day for thirty days, it will become a habit.

Look at other aspects of your life that cause anxiety. It may not just be a lack of sales. There may be double (or more) stress points. LIST ALL OF YOUR CAUSES.

Plugging five or six things into one electrical outlet will blow a fuse. It's the same with you. Identify the real causes and unplug a few things by taking them out of your daily routine.

SUCCESS TACTIC: After taking action, you must still "let the worry go" mentally. The secret is to simply release it by smiling. Your smile has the power to turn a negative into a positive, and expel the worry from your system.

FINAL NOTE: It is critical for you to realize that stress and worry are not someone else's fault. You bring it on yourself. There is only one sure thing you can get from worry and stress…a heart attack. The alternative is much better for you, and much more fun.

What books should be in my library? What are best tapes and CDs to listen to in the car?

The reason I want you to *own* these books is that after you read them, you can continue to use them for reference. It's not just your library -- it's your *reference* library.

SOME OF MY FAVORITE BOOKS:

How to Win Friends and Influence People by Dale Carnegie

How to Stop Worrying and Start Living by Dale Carnegie

Think and Grow Rich by Napoleon Hill

Acres of Diamonds by Russell Conwell

Psycho Cybernetics by Maxwell Maltz

Magic of Thinking Big by David Schwartz

OUT-OF-PRINT FAVORITE BOOKS THAT WILL BE MORE DIFFICULT TO FIND:

How to Sell Your Way Through Life by Napoleon Hill

Keys to Success and Personal Efficiency by Orison Swett Marden

He Can Who Thinks He Can by Orison Swett Marden

Selling Things by Orison Swett Marden

Autobiography of P.T. Barnum by P.T. Barnum

The New Art of Selling by Elmer Leterman

You can find out-of-print books on the Internet by searching www.ABEBooks.com or www.bookfinder.com by either title or author. You don't have to buy a first edition. You don't have to buy a signed edition. You DO have to buy, own, and read a cheap edition.

SOME OF MY FAVORITE CDS:

The Art of Exceptional Living by Jim Rohn

Success Through a Positive Mental Attitude by Napoleon Hill and W. Clement Stone

The Strangest Secret by Earl Nightingale

Lead the Field by Earl Nightingale

FINAL ANSWER: Once you begin to build and read your own success library, you'll simultaneously begin to build your education, and enhance your personal development. For years Charlie "Tremendous" Jones has used the quote, "The only difference from where you are right now, and where you'll be one year from now, are the books you read and the people you meet." He is correct.

Your job is to meet the right people and read the right books.

As long as I'm quoting other people, let me give you this famous Harvey Mackay quote, "Don't read a book, study it." Every book on my list is worth studying.

Should I change jobs?

If you're asking me that question, the answer is: *You probably should*. If you're thinking about it, one of 6.5 things is wrong:

1. You don't believe in your company.

2. You don't believe in your product.

3. You believe your competition's product is better than yours.

4. You don't like your co-workers.

5. You don't like your boss.

6. You're not making enough sales.

6.5 You don't like anything or anybody. You're angry.

I'm writing this about a sales job, but it applies to any job. If you're thinking about changing jobs, it's merely a justification for what you've already decided. It's like when you decide you're not in love anymore. You may be there physically, but mentally, you're gone.

People change jobs all the time. There's nothing wrong with it, *unless* you haven't carefully considered where you're moving to, or deeper -- what's really causing you to want to move.

The short answer to "Should I change jobs?" is:

Become the best where you already are, and then move up.

If you leave disgruntled, it's likely you'll be disgruntled someplace else. If you leave a winner, it's likely you'll be a winner someplace else.

Take the time to examine why you're thinking about leaving. Make a list of every reason (big or small). You might just be unhappy because of your office conditions, but it may be that your company doesn't support you. In my experience I have found that it's never one reason -- it's a series of reasons. (Company's cheap, customers are unhappy, boss is a jerk, I'm underappreciated, I'm underpaid.)

One other caution: Take your time and make a deliberate plan to move into a job that you could love. The main reason people leave their job is that they don't love it. Think about it. Why would you work someplace for eight or nine hours a day and not love it. That's crazy.

Now some of you are thinking: "Jeffrey, you don't understand, my mortgage payment. I make a lot of money in this job. My family." I understand. Just keep working on it until you crack.

If you want or need to move, move with a winning record of success, move with a plan, and move to something you love.

Should I sign a non-compete?

No you should not, but you may be forced to.
If you're entering a new job, and everyone else is signing non-competes, your choice may be "sign it, or you can't work here."

If you do sign a non-compete, I would be exceptionally careful. Some are enforceable, some are not. Some companies only put them there as a deterrent. Some actually try to enforce them.

If you have a lawyer that you can run your contract by, I would do it. After all, they had their legal department prepare it, you might want to have your lawyer take a look at it.

CAUTION: If you're asked to sign a non-compete contract in the middle of your employment, don't. I'm not a lawyer. I can't give legal advice. But if your company all of a sudden springs a non-compete on you, and you've been there for months or years, something is drastically wrong.

The goal is for employers and salespeople to gain a better understanding and respect for one another, so that the end result will be what they both desire: more sales.

Here's my solution that I believe is fair for all. The employer should require that if the salesperson for any reason leaves:

1. That he or she not discuss internal trade secrets or divulge company strategies.

2. That he or she leave behind all documentation, computer databases, and anything pertaining to the company, or its product, or its customers.

3. That any of the company's existing customers or those in the current pipeline (especially those being worked on by the salesperson) be untouchable.

I would ask both employers and salespeople to seek out a way that both are protected, and that there is mutual respect at the beginning of their relationship, so that the end result matches their beginning expectations. If the first thing a salesperson has to sign is the, "I don't trust you clause," then the last thing the employer is going to get is the undying loyalty that they are hoping for.

FINAL ANSWER: If the non-compete is fair to everyone then it can and should be signed. This gives everyone a total understanding of what should happen, during and after, your employment. The key is that it be fair to everyone.

Free Red⬆Bit: Want more information before you sign your non-compete? Go to www.gitomer.com, register if you are a first time user, and enter the words NON-COMPETE in the RedBit box.

PART TWO

Prospecting for Golden Leads and Making Solid Appointments

How do I make a cold call?

There are two kinds of cold calls: on the phone, and in person.

On the phone, you have to get by a gatekeeper or voice mail. You do this by saying, "Hi, my name is Jeffrey, and I'd like to speak to Mr. Jones. It's a business matter of a personal nature."

When you get to Mr. Jones, you give your first name, and you ask an engaging question. If you're selling cell phones, you would ask something like, "What are the three most underutilized, yet most profitable methods of using a cell phone?"

The secret of the cold call is "engage," not "make the sale."

The object of a cold call is to set an appointment.

After the prospect answers your question (or you answer it for them), you would say, "I have several other important, little known, profitable facts about cellular phones. I'd like to meet with you for a few minutes to talk about how you can take advantage of them."

It's getting harder and harder to make an actual cold call, in person, with all the security issues. If you're calling on a big company, you're not gonna get in (unless you scam your way in). If you're calling on a small company, you can be truthful -- or you can be elusive. Truthful would be, "I'd like to speak to the person in charge of computer profitability." More elusive might be, "I have an important question about company morale, based on computer operations, and I'd like to speak to the person in charge of morale."

The key here is that I've asked for someone in charge of nothing. The more you ask for someone, that no one can define, the better chance you have of speaking to a boss, or a decision maker, because the gatekeeper, having no idea what to say, but having direct access to the boss, will buzz him or her.

FINAL ANSWER: Let me repeat that the secret to cold calling is *engagement*. If you're fortunate enough to get to that decision maker, you better have a damn good question to ask.

> If you ask me the biggest
> secret of cold calling,
> I would tell you in one word.
> Preparation.
> If you're no good at it,
> I can sum it up in two words.
> Preparation-H.

How can I STOP making cold calls and still make appointments?

No one likes cold calls. Not the salesperson who makes them. And surely not the prospect who receives them. It's a way to sell -- just not the best way to sell. And it's getting worse by the day.

Here are 6.5 ways to professionally cure the common cold call and still get appointments. The principle behind each way is simple -- **Put yourself in front of people who can say yes to you, and deliver value first.** Value that generates attraction to get them to call you.

1. Write an article. One that gets in front of your key prospects and customers.

2. Get on a talk show. Call in if you have to, but it's better to be interviewed.

3. Give a speech. At an association meeting or trade show.

4. Send an e-idea of the week. To your customer, prospect, and influence list.

5. Hold a free seminar. Make the topic compelling, and the content dynamic.

6. Network at a business function. Be seen by those who count and those who decide. Get to know your customers personally.

6.5 Get a referral from someone who loves you. Referrals beat cold calls -- 100 to 1.

But in case you're wondering: Here are some acceptable cold call circumstances:

☎ After a sales call, go to one or two neighboring businesses or offices. **BEST WAY:** Try to get your customer to introduce you rather than busting in alone.

☎ Make a small set number of calls a day to practice gaining engagement or try out new sales ideas. Using the cold call as training. Cold calls are a lousy way to make a sale -- but they are a great place to learn how to sell.

☎ Calling a particular category of business that has proven successful in the past or is "hot." If everyone else is buying, engagement will be easier. Take a testimonial or three with you.

FINAL ANSWER: The secret of cold calling is -- it's not who you know -- it's who knows you. If they know you, they will invite you in. If they don't know you, you're toast. The hard part is getting known -- but it can be done.

I challenge you to become better known. I challenge you to become more valued in your business community. And, I challenge you to create a better marketing outreach program than the one you have. If you do -- they will call you. And that call is HOT!

How can I get around a lower-level person?

OBVIOUS ANSWER: Never go to the lower-level person to begin with.

The higher you start, the easier it is to get to a real decision maker. The only reason that salespeople go to a lower-level person is because they think it's an easier level of entry. When in fact, it complicates everything.

GOOD ANSWER: If you have made the mistake of "going lower-level," and need to move up the ladder, say to the lower-level person, "I have a list of a half a dozen questions that I would like to ask you and Bill, (or you and your boss) and I was wondering if it would be possible to set that meeting within the next few days."

BETTER ANSWER: The easiest way to get around the lower-level person is to include them. This way they don't feel threatened.

WORST-CASE SCENARIO: The lower-level person is blocking you from getting to the higher-level person. This is found in spineless, corporate, political environments. In other words, the lower-level idiot that you're talking to is refusing to do the best for his company. Instead, he is doing whatever he can to maintain his meager, political presence.

BEST ANSWER: (And my recommendation) Get to a higher-level person by means of higher-level information. You can't get to a higher-level person with the same information that you presented to the lower-level person.

You have to go in with a white paper, full of ideas to positively affect your prospects productivity and profitability. You have to go in with an article that you just wrote in their industry-related publication. You have to go in with critical information. Critical information that doesn't interest the lower-level person, but that is crucial to the higher-level person.

High-level people want to make a profit. Low-level people insist on saving money.

IMPORTANT NOTE: Don't throw the lower-level person under the bus (even though it's tempting as hell). Just say that you have information that you consider crucial to the higher-level person, and that you wanted to deliver it to him personally. When you meet with the higher-level person, close the sale as fast as you can because I guarantee you that the lower-level sniveler will do everything he or she can to puke all over your birthday cake.

What is the best way to get information to a prospect?

ANSWER: Bring them an idea that helps them build their business.

What were you thinking here? Did you think I was gonna tell you how to deliver your self-serving, waste of time literature?

SALES BALLS: If you're gonna send your brochure, send it in a trash can. Save the prospect some time. Make sure you have your logo screen printed on the outside of the trash can.

Write a little note to the customer saying, "You were probably going to put it in the trash can anyway, so I saved you a step and put it in the trash can for you. Hopefully you'll treat everyone equally, and throw all of my competitor's brochures in here as well."

Continue the note by saying, "I have a few ideas I'd like to run by you that I'm certain you won't want to throw away. And I'd appreciate 15 or 20 minutes of your time so that I might be able to share them with you."

The BEST way to get information to a prospect is to make the information a "must read" once it's in the door.

What is the best way to get past the gatekeeper?

19

The gatekeeper, a person everyone in sales needs to "get past" in order to enter a company and potentially find a decision maker, is one of the biggest barriers in sales. And the reason is, salespeople think they're smarter than the gatekeeper -- when actually the reverse is true.

That gatekeeper has heard every sales line in the world. Ten times. And she can smell a sales skunk before they even enter the door. He or she also knows when you're being sincere or insincere, and will not tolerate a condescending manner, or an impatient know-it-all.

How do I know this to be true? In my early days of selling, it was part of my "come-uppence" training.

I have 10.5 ideas of what you can do to get past the gatekeeper:

1. Know the name of the decision maker before you call.

2. Have a response for, "What's this in reference to?" My standard response for years has been: "It's a business matter of a personal nature."

3. Be friendly.

4. Ask for help (What's the best time? When does he usually…).

5. Be sincere.

6. Don't try worn out sales tactics.

7. If at all possible, tell the truth.

8. Have a real good reason for calling beyond wanting to sell something.

9. Send an e-mail greeting prior to making the phone call. (Yes, Sparky, this may be a little hard to do because you don't know the e-mail address, but you can always call someone and ask, or just send a fax.)

10. Be original. If you don't put a twist on your words and make the gatekeeper think, "Wow, this guy is cool," you'll be relegated to the usual list of excuses gatekeepers are employed to give. ("He's in a meeting." "He doesn't see people without an appointment.") You know, the usual.

10.5 They've heard it before. Whatever kind of ploy you're thinking about trying. Whatever kind of phony line you're thinking about delivering, I can promise you the gatekeeper will smell it and throw you out like a three-day-old fish.

Be aware that bosses will often
ask gatekeepers what they thought
of the salesperson. The gatekeepers
thinking will often determine your fate.

FINAL ANSWER: Getting around the gatekeeper needs to be a positive experience. If it's not positive, be certain that the gatekeeper will announce your presence to the boss by saying, "some sales jerk is on line three."

What is the best way to get information on a prospect before a sales appointment?

The best, fastest, and most accurate way of getting information on a customer is right on the Internet.

1. Go to the customer's Web site. Print out several of the most important pages for use later. Read them. Make notes.

2. Go to www.google.com. Google the name of the company you're going to meet. Google (or a comparable search engine like www.dogpile.com) will lead you to media information about the company.

3. You may even want to go to the archives of the *Business Journal*. (www.bizjournals.com) Do a quick search on the company name.

4. Google the name of the person you're meeting.
If nothing pops up, you may want to Google the name of their mommy or daddy. If you can't find anything on the person you're meeting with, go back to their Web site and find out the name of the person's boss. That's the person you *should* be meeting with. Do a little research. Print out their bio page. Read all their literature and make a few red-lines, write down ideas, and jot down a few questions that you'll want to ask as a result of the information you have just found.

When the customer sees that you have gone to the trouble of going to their Web site and printed out pages of pertinent information, their respect level for you will increase by one thousand percent.

They will immediately engage with you because you pre-engaged with them.

FINAL ANSWER:

Everything you need to know about a customer has been written by them or about them. And it lives on the Internet. All you have to do is uncover it. *And use it.*

What is the best way to set an appointment?

BEST WAY: Face to face.

SECOND BEST WAY: On the phone, through their administrative assistant. (This means you're meeting with a big-wig.)

THIRD BEST WAY: Via e-mail.

Well, instead of me droning on about traditional methods, let's shoot for the moon. Here's how to get to the CEO eight out of 10 times. *But*, it's hard work. *But*, you will win.

SALES BALLS ANSWER: Using the Second Best Way (the phone) -- tell the CEO's assistant you want to interview the boss for an ezine you're doing every month on leadership. Tell the assistant that the newsletter is sent out to five thousand influential people. Tell the assistant that you want to know what's a good time to conduct a 30-minute interview -- and that you'll be bringing a photographer. The assistant won't know what the hell to do! But I guarantee you this method will work 80-100% of the time.

MINOR PROBLEM: You have to have the ezine and the mailing list first. The good news is, this is part of being best. Do you read my weekly e-mail magazine Sales Caffeine? Am I reading yours?

This approach will make you an immediate winner in the mind of the customer, make getting an appointment with the big boss a piece of cake, and establish you as a leader.

FINAL ANSWER: When you're in the interview, don't pitch your product -- and only talk about yourself if he asks. Share the value you have provided for others. Try to make an appointment to come back and pitch your stuff *after* the article that you wrote about him appears.

FINAL WIN: When the boss gets your ezine with his photo and leadership philosophy, who do you think he'll forward it to? Correct! Everybody and their dog.

How do I find out who the real decision maker is?

THE SHORT ANSWER IS: Start with the biggest boss. Sometimes called an owner. Sometimes called a chief executive officer, and euphemistically called, the person that pulls the trigger. *The* decision-maker.

Too often salespeople start too low and have to beg their way, or worm their way, up the ladder. I get e-mails all the time asking me, "How do I get around a lower-level person?" And the answer is, don't start there.

Why would you start with someone who can't decide?

The key is to get to the highest-level person possible. You can find out exactly who they are by going to their Web site, or using a research tool like Hoover's. This will allow you to know who they are.

And then the question is, do they know you? Because, if they don't know you, it's less likely that they will perceive enough value to meet with you.

Here are three quick ways to get known:

1. Write an article that they would read.

2. Give a speech that they might listen to. The easiest place is your association meetings.

3. Create a way to interview them for an article that you would write about them. Something on leadership or business philosophy.

CAUTION: It ain't easy. I'm giving you answers here that may take you years to perfect. But once you do, you will forever be in a leadership position, and you will have forever created the law of attraction to yourself.

The key is not to "call the decision maker." The key is to "have the decision maker call you."

FINAL ANSWER: The first success key is to get in front of the real decision maker with a value message. Something you wrote. Writing makes you look smart -- and valuable. Millions of people will be reading this answer. Some of them may even want to call me when they're done reading this answer, because they want their salespeople to call on more decision makers and less purchasing agents. That someone may even be you. My number is 704-333-1112. I'm standing by.

What do I do when the prospect doesn't show for an appointment?

23

How many times have you made an appointment with a customer or prospect, only to arrive and be told that he or she is not available, or had something else come up? Rats.

Maybe:

1. They forgot.

2. Something unavoidable happened.

3. They were making a sale themselves.

4. You weren't important -- as a vendor.

5. There is no perceived need -- or, no established need -- for you.

6. You haven't established enough interest.

7. The prospect does not respect salespeople.

8. The prospect is a rude butthead.

8.5 They perceived little or no value in meeting with you.

Besides swearing under your breath and biting your tongue, what's the best way to react?

When the prospect fails to show, you have a power position. Take the "no-show" seriously, but don't take it personally.

Don't let it get to your attitude. Don't get mad. Don't say stupid things. Don't burn the bridge. Many salespeople get on their high horse, and lose the respect of the buyer -- and the potential for the order. Don't let this be you. The "no-show" opportunity works best when implemented at once. Follow up immediately with this strategy:

Blame yourself first. Try to help them save face. Begin by saying that you must have made a mistake on the meeting time and venue, or else surely they would have been present (especially if the appointment was confirmed). Let them off the hook.

Make like it's no big deal. But make them feel as guilty as you can.

Listen to their lame excuse empathetically. After listening to the customer's excuse, ask for another meeting as close to today as possible.

Set the next meeting to your best advantage. Try to make the meeting at your office or a neutral site (a restaurant is best).

Agree on the ground-rules for another change. Let them know that if something comes up, a (cell) phone call would be greatly appreciated.

FINAL ANSWER: If the prospect doesn't show, make it a positive. Your objective is make the sale -- not make a scene. If you want the prospect to show the *first* time, make sure there's value for them. If you want them to show the *second* time, make sure there's value for them. Get it?

No value -- no show.

What do I do when the prospect lies?

24

Understand why they did it. Determine whether it's a money lie or a business lie. But realize that all lies are bad. Some are just worse than others. Most lies prospects will tell you are money lies that "pit you against the other guy." Lies like: Can you match this price? They'll do more than you'll do. They said they'd throw in freight. They said they could deliver faster.

All are non-relationship building. If you want to do business with liars, it's your choice. But I can tell you that if someone lies about one thing -- odds are they'll lie about something else. Like: Lost the invoice. Check's in the mail. I thought you said… That's not what we agreed on. And so on.

The best way to do business with a liar is confront them with the truth. Tell them that you do business as a partner, not a vendor. If they really want to do business with you, a few dollars worth of freight, or a few pennies off the price, pales in comparison to the value of your product, the correctness of delivery, and the service after the sale.

SALES BALLS: If your lying customer still can't see the light, tell him that you may not be the best choice for business, and that you think you have someone that can serve him better. Then, refer him to the competitor that you hate the most.

FINAL ANSWER: If they lie once, they'll lie twice. Be aware of the snake you sleep with. You may wake up with a bitten asp.

What questions am I asking my prospects and customers that my competition isn't asking?

You're probably asking dumb questions like, "What's important to you?" "What keeps you up at night?" "Who are you using right now?" "Do you have a budget?" "Do you have a contract?" and other moronic questions about their wallet -- that in my opinion -- are none of your business. I'd certainly tell you that if you asked me.

The key to questioning lies in your ability to differentiate from those who have preceded you. What can you ask that none of the others have asked? What can you ask that makes you appear smarter, and better, than your competition? What can you ask that makes your customer stop and think, consider new information, and respond in terms of you?

At the core of your business success are your differentiating questions.

The easiest way to find a few questions is to look at your product or service from an ownership standpoint, rather than a purchase standpoint. "Mr. Jones, after you purchase this car, where is the first place you're going to drive it?" or "Who will you show first?" or "Where will you take your first family road trip?" Not only are these great questions, it makes the prospect think in terms of, "I already own it."

Then think about the customer's past history, or the customer's existing knowledge of your product or service, and ask questions that draw on their experience and their expertise. Begin questions with phrases like, "How have you found…?" or "What's been your experience…?" or "In your opinion…?"

Too many salespeople (not you of course) drone on about their product without ever knowing the customer's opinion, and it's that kind of ignorance that allows your competition to come in and beat you. Not with price. Beat you with questions.

PERSONAL GUARANTEE:

I guarantee you that more sales are lost with poor questions and poor salesmanship than are lost to lowest price.

START HERE: Make a list of the 10 questions you think are most powerful. And put a check mark by the ones you believe it is probable that your competition is also asking. Don't be discouraged if you check off 8 out of 10 (and the other 2 were maybes).

Now make another list, and another list, and another list, until you begin to develop insightful, intelligent, emotionally engaging questions that don't just differentiate you from your competition, but rather beat them into the ground.

Why did the last five prospects say no? What am I doing about it?

Most of the time when a prospect says "no" salespeople accept it, and leave. Most of the time when a prospect tells you why they said no, they're not telling the truth.

The biggest cause of sales rejection in the mind of the salesperson is, "My price was too high." It's also the easiest excuse for a buyer to give in order to make the salesperson go away.

Other than price, there are 5.5 big reasons you lost the sale:

1. The customer believed you were not the best choice.

2. The customer had a previous experience they weren't happy with.

3. The customer has a personal relationship with another vendor. And just an FYI – price is not a consideration when a personal relationship exists.

4. You have not shown any differentiation between your product or service and the other guy's product or service, therefore price is all that's left.

5. You have not shown the customer how they profit more or produce more as a result of owning your products or service. When there's no value, price is all that's left.

5.5 You tried to make the sale by yourself. Let's face it, Sparky, you're not that good at this yet. Why aren't you bringing along a customer as a testimonial to prove that what you're saying is true? Why aren't you bringing along a customer as a testimonial to prove that price doesn't matter? Why aren't you bringing along a customer as a testimonial to prove that you are who you say you are?

FINAL ANSWER: Combine why you lost the last 5 sales, and how you made the last 5 sales, and add testimonials to the mix. The knowledge it adds to your sales power will blow the price objection out of the water.

"You already know how to make every sale, you're just not using your own sales power."

-- Jeffrey Gitomer

Why did the last 10 prospects say yes? How am I building on that?

The last 10 sales will show you the eleventh. Capture and repeat your success habits. Easy concept. So easy it's never used.

Salespeople (you included) continue to fight the same battles sale after sale. Price too high, can't get an appointment, satisfied with present supplier, taking three bids, can't reach the decision maker, blah, blah, blah.

I have an idea for you. Study history. No, not American history. You don't care who Franklin Pierce's Vice President was, do you?

Study your own history. Your sales history. Just go back to:

- ★ Your last 10 leads.
- ★ Your last 10 appointments.
- ★ Your last 10 sales calls.
- ★ Your last 10 sales.
- ★ Your last 10 repeat sales.
- ★ Your last 10 referrals.
- ★ Your last 10 lost sales.
- ★ Your last 10 calls for service help.
- ★ Your last 10 customer complaints.
- ★ Your last 10 lost customers.
- ★ Your last 10 testimonials.

That's enough history to predict the future. Actually it's enough history to *alter* the future. Your future. That's enough information to cure all your ills, and double your sales.

OK, maybe you need to do the list with 25 of each, but that sounds like work. And salespeople aren't willing to do the hard work it takes to make sales easy. Ten sounds like a more workable number. Start there.

This concept has certainly opened my eyes to the probability of making future sales by studying sales history. It's a strategy you can implement. And one you can make more sales from.

DEEPER THOUGHT: After you ask yourself the surface questions, ask deeper "why" questions and *list* the answers. The reason for the list is to spot the trend and figure out how to eliminate the mistakes, conserve time and money, prevent the problems from re-occurring, and focus your energy on what has been successful. WOW!

Why haven't you done this before? It's so obvious, you overlooked it. So did I.

Free Red Bit: Want to learn more about how to question your last ten sales? Go to www.gitomer.com, register if you are a first time user, and enter the words LAST TEN in the RedBit box.

PART THREE

How to Win the Sales Battle AND the Sales War

THE CUSTOMER
WAS WRONG,
AND I PROVED IT.

YEAH, AND ALL IT COST
YOU WAS THE SALE.

What is the best way to approach a sale?

I'm against all systems of selling. So are all salespeople. But the reason I'm against selling systems is that they're all manipulative. They're all "me-based." They're all too rigid. And the worst thing about them is that they force the salesperson to think: "Where am I in the system?" vs. "How am I helping this person in his or her desire to purchase what I've got?"

So what's a salesperson to do? **Develop a strategy, develop an approach, and develop the ability to engage the other person in a way that grabs his interest -- so you don't have to worry about a system. Build a *structure* -- not a system. Build a *strategy* -- not a system.**

If you think about the logical, sequential order of a sales structure, it involves:

➤➤ **Making a connection.**

➤➤ **Making an appointment.**

➤➤ **Getting ready for the sale.**

➤➤ **Engaging the prospect in a way that you gain his interest.**

➤➤ **Proving the value of your offer.**

➤➤ **Coming to some kind of an agreement.**

➤➤ **Delivering.**

➤➤ **Servicing.**

➤➤ **Creating an environment that's so phenomenal that the customer is compelled to buy from you again, refer other people to you, and speak about you positively in the marketplace.**

Master those elements, and the world is your commission.

Now that seems pretty simple, doesn't it? Just add two words to this formula, and you'll become a billionaire. Have you guessed the two words yet? They're two words that most salespeople don't want to hear: HARD WORK.

No ultra-successful salesperson becomes ultra-successful without ultra-hard work.

Let me take this process one step higher. The process of approach, strategy, and structure is driven by philosophy. Your philosophy will determine your structure. How you think about, feel about, and live the practices of your sales life will be reflected in your philosophy.

My sales philosophy is:

1. **I give value first.**

2. **I help other people.**

3. **I strive to do my best at what I love.**

4. **I establish long-term relationships with everyone.**

5. **I have fun -- and I have fun every day.**

This philosophy set the stage for my success. Living my philosophy makes me a better salesperson -- and a better person. Do you have a philosophy? Do you have a structure? Create both and you will set the stage for a quantum leap forward. Or, you can wallow in your system.

What are the two most killer questions in sales? **29**

SECOND MOST KILLER: *"Mr. Jones, when buying (insert your product here), what are the three biggest mistakes people make?"*

Fear of loss is greater than desire to gain. People don't want to make mistakes, especially on a large purchase.

There are variations to this question. You can substitute, "three biggest opportunities" or, "three biggest reasons." The key is to create a deficit between you and the probable purchaser. Ask a question that you know the answer to (and they don't).

MOST KILLER: *"Mr. Jones, when I say* (insert your product, your company, or anything you want an opinion about here) ***what one word comes to mind?"***

Example: "Mr. Jones, when I say 'copy machine,' what one word comes to mind?" Mr. Jones replies. "Lousy service!" You say, "Mr. Jones, that's two words, I was wanting one word."

This is the most powerful question because it not only gives you top of mind awareness (the customer "hot button"), it also tells you their attitude towards it.

CAUTION: Both of these questions require mastery. I can pretty much assure you that the first dozen times you use these questions, they will not yield you the results you're hoping for. But I can also assure you that these questions WORK!

What are the three dumbest questions in sales?

30

THIRD DUMBEST: *"Have you ever heard of us?"*
If you have to ask this question, it means you're probably trying to make certain that your prospect has not had a bad experience, or knows anything bad about you. Your reputation will generally arrive before you do. If something bad has happened in the past, your prospect will bring it up. If you have to ask this question, you're probably not very well-known anyway.

SECOND DUMBEST: *"Can you tell me a little bit about your company?"* This question means that you were either too lazy or too stupid to go to the Internet and find out about them. Don't ask any questions that you couldn't have gone on the Internet and found out the answer to yourself. When you force your customer to answer questions already known, they become bored and disengaged. And it is potentially the poorest reflection on you.

And now the granddaddy of all stupidity…

THE DUMBEST QUESTION IN SALES: (You should know it, you ask it all the time.) *"What will it take to get your business?"* It's most likely that you have asked this question dozens of times. And all you're asking the prospect is, "How low do you want me to drop my pants, er, I mean price, in order to get this order?"

Now let me ask *you* a question. Have you been in sales
for longer than one week? Don't you *know* what it will take
to get their business? And wouldn't it be one thousand times
better for you to walk into a sales call and say, "Mr. Jones,
I've been talking to your people, your customers, and your
vendors, and I believe I've uncovered *exactly* what it will
take to get your business. I'm going to run a few ideas by
you, and all I ask is, if you like the ideas, that we begin
doing business with one another. Fair enough?"

If you walk in *asking* what it will take to get their business,
you will either leave empty handed, or you will get the
order but have no profit. Either way, you're a loser.

If you walk in **knowing** what it will take to get their
business, it's most likely you will walk out with the order.

BIG SECRET:

"Knowing what it will take"
to get someone's business
is one of the least used
and most powerful techniques
to getting new business.
Your job is not to use this technique.
Your job is to master it.

What is the best way to control a phone conversation?

Two words: **Ask questions.**

The person who asks the question has the control. If you make a statement, follow it up with a question. The cool part about this answer is that it's a double benefit.

BENEFIT 1: You're in control.
BENEFIT 2: The person answering you is giving you the valuable information you need to make the sale and build the relationship.

My personal belief is that if you ask enough of the right questions, you don't have to make many statements.

Telling is selling.
Asking is buying.

If you know me, you know my sales mantra:
People don't like to be sold, but they love to buy.

Let's get back to control for a minute. Once you know the secret: asking questions equals phone control, you can do what is known as "dangle control." You can chatter back and forth, even let the prospect ask some questions, always knowing you can take control back with a single question.

SIDE NOTE: On the phone, I like to ask thought provoking questions that let the customer feel good, yet thought-challenged. I'll ask questions that start with, "What's been your experience…?" or "How has this helped your profit?" or "How have you successfully used…?" This gives the person on the other end a chance to think and feel challenged, not provoked or irked.

I ask the prospect for his or her wisdom.

Phone control is not important, it's critical. Control of the phone leads to control of the sale. Control of the sale leads to control of the wallet. Your wallet.

"TO PLACE AN ORDER IMMEDIATELY AND SPARE YOURSELF A 45-MINUTE HIGH-PRESSURE SALES PITCH, PRESS 1."

How do I get around the price objection? (Who brought up price, anyway?)

The good part is that price objection indicates buyer interest. Asking, "How much is it?" is THE BIGGEST buying signal. Telling me, "Your price is too high," is THE SECOND BIGGEST buying signal. The problem is that you are so anxious to make the sale, you're willing to compromise the price just to "get the sale."

Too often salespeople (not you of course) have already given their price in advance of the prospect asking for it. This is a HUGE strategic disadvantage to the salesperson. Why give the price in advance? If the prospect is interested, he never gets a chance to ask, "How much?" Why do salespeople give away their own strength?

Well, I have discovered a strategy that will win the sale at your price more often than not. And it's easier than you think.

PRICE ANSWER THAT ELIMINATES "YOUR PRICE IS TOO HIGH":
If the customer asks how much it is, reply by asking permission to ask a question first (a qualifying question). Then ask a series of quick questions that lead to a price offering that assures purchase.

HERE'S THE CONCEPT: Define need, desire, and status first. And then be CERTAIN they perceive value. Why give the price without seeing how high the interest level is? Once you know their interest level, you must establish the value of the product before you ask for the sale.

Have a solid reason for the price. Then say, "Our prices are fair and firm." I could just say our prices are "firm" but I added "fair" to soften the blow, and then establish their value.

In the battle for price, every word counts. It's psychological warfare and perceived value as much as anything. As a seller you have to know the psychology, know the "why, how long, what's prevented?" things of the issue. And then build value that leads to purchase.

HINT: If the customer won't buy, it's not their fault.

HERE'S THE STRATEGY: Ask questions to qualify need and desire. Give a statement about you and the product that sets up the price as final. And when you deliver the price, ask for the sale in the same breath.

HERE'S THE LESSON: Salespeople are not needed for the purpose of quoting a price. They are the bridge between the selling price, and the perception of value provided to earn the sale. And it all starts when the prospect says, "How much is it?"

FINAL ANSWER: Don't "get around it." Be proud of your price. THE ONLY SURE WAY TO BEAT, "Your price is too high," is to use a customer (video) testimonial or two to support it. Testimonials are the BEST way to beat down the price objection and win the sale.

What is the difference between a stall and an objection?

Two answers: A stall is, "I want to think about it," or "I have to meet with other people." An objections is, "Your price is too high," or "We have a satisfactory supply." Both are put-offs which basically say, "You haven't sold me yet."

Maybe they perceive too high a risk.

Maybe they think they can get it someplace cheaper.

Maybe they don't have enough confidence in you to go forward.

Maybe they are not the decision maker.

You haven't proven enough value. You haven't shown enough difference between you and your competition. And you certainly have not gained the trust of the buyer to invest his money in your product or your service.

Most salespeople are foolish enough to take a stall or an objection as the real reason for a sale not moving forward. Objections or barriers of any kind are an indication from the customer that they want to buy, they just may not want to buy from you.

Even if a customer says, "I'm not interested," (probably the most classic turn-off objection other than slamming the phone down or throwing you out) it's an indication that you have not engaged them.

The bottom line is conversion. You have to convert their lack of confidence, their lack of trust, and their lack of perceived value into a sale.

FINAL ANSWER: A stall is easier to convert. An objection may take a bit more work. BUT both must be qualified as the real reason for not purchasing now. Most are false reasons. The master salesperson must ask why these are occurring to get to the real sales-block.

Free Red Bit: Want to know the keys to overcoming objections? Go to www.gitomer.com, register if you are a first time user, and enter the word OBJECTION in the RedBit box.

How can I prevent objections from occurring?

34

ANSWER: Cover them in your presentation.

You have not had a new objection since your career began. You already know the 10 objections your customer is going to throw at you.

"I'm satisfied with who I got," "Your price is too high," "My home office handles that," and other lame customer excuses ad nauseam.

You have two choices when preventing an objection:

1. Somewhere in your presentation you say, "You know, Mr. Prospect, a lot of people tell us our prices are too high, before they become customers. I would like to share a few testimonials with you before we get too deep into our conversation. These are people who thought our prices were too high initially, bought anyway, and have been our customer for years."

2. Try to prevent it yourself. "You know, Mr. Prospect, some people tell me that my prices are too high, but it's because they don't quite understand the full value of our product, which over time, is actually lower in cost. I'll demonstrate this a little later, but please have confidence that I would not be so foolish as to waste your time if I were not the best value."

Either one of these preventions will work.

FINAL ANSWER:

Personally, I believe the testimonial to be the strongest sales tool you can possess.

Either way, your job is to identify the 10 most common objections that you get, create best responses for them, and figure out how to put them in your sales presentation so that at the end, you're more likely to get a signature on a contract.

How do I recognize buying signals? What is the most powerful buying signal?

The link between the presentation and the close are buying signals given by your prospect. As a professional salesperson, your job is to recognize a buying signal and convert it into a sale. Recognizing is the hard part.

Recognizing signals to buy is one of the "art" areas in the science of selling. Listen to the buyer. He or she will give you signals. As you give your presentation, the buyer will gesture, question, play with your product, or in some way communicate that he is inclined to purchase. When you hear a buying signal, that's your signal to ask for the sale.

RULE OF THUMB: Any question asked by the prospect must be considered a buying signal.

THE MOST POWERFUL BUYING SIGNAL is when your prospect asks: "How much is it?" It means you have peaked enough interest to get the prospect to think "ownership," and want to know how affordable it is.

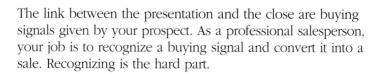

Free Red Bit: Want to learn the 21.5 buying signals to look for? Go to www.gitomer.com, register if you are a first time user, and enter the word SIGNALS in the RedBit box.

What is the best time and the best way to ask for the sale?

To get the sale -- you must ask for it! "Yes, Jeffrey," you say, "but *when* do you ask? What's the perfect time to ask?"

How do I know? No one knows that except you. I can only tell you it's a delicate combination of the prospect's buying signals and your gut feeling.

How to ask and *what to ask* are easier to define than *when to ask*. Since the "ask" is a critical part of the sale, you'd better be prepared with a number of options for the how and what part.

IMPORTANT NOTE: Here's what *never* to ask: "What will it take for me to get your business?" or "What will it take to earn your business?" That's an insult question. Great salespeople figure out what it takes, and then do it.

MORE IMPORTANT NOTE: Many salespeople are "ask reluctant." I refer to them as "sales-chickens." If this is you, just realize the worst that can happen when you ask is that the prospect says "no" -- which to any good salesperson means "not yet!" Big deal.

How do you ask for the sale? Here are 7.5 ways:

1. Ask -- What's the risk? When you ask the prospect what risks are associated in doing business with you, real objections surface -- or -- (and here's the best part) there are usually none that come to mind. You say, "Well, Mr. Johnson, when would you like to start not risking?" and the sale is yours.

2. Ask -- When is the next job? If you're making a sale where there are lots of opportunities (printer, supplies, temp help, construction, graphic design) you only need to get one job (order) to prove yourself.

3. Ask for an indirect commitment. Could you arrange your schedule to be there at delivery? How many people will need to be trained? When can we set up training?

4. Ask -- What's preventing it? Is there anything preventing you from doing business with us? What's in the way? What are the obstacles?

5. If there's an obstacle or objection. **Ask -- Is that the only reason?** In other words, Mr. Johnson, if it wasn't for (objection) then could we move forward?

6. Ask or communicate creatively. Go to the 5¢ & 10¢ store (pretty much dates me doesn't it) and buy some plastic fence and a few plastic (rubber) people. Wire one person to the fence that most resembles (or would be non-offensive to) the prospect. Send it in a box to the prospect -- and include a flyer declaring it's "National Get Off the Fence Week." Tell the prospect he's been thinking about it long enough -- and what better time to get off the fence, and place an order than during this special celebration week? Tell him he'll be helping underprivileged salespeople all over the world by getting off the fence and placing an order. Create some laughter. Have some fun. Make some sales.

7. Create an offer so good that you can end by asking, "Fair enough?" "Mr. Johnson, I don't know if we can help you or not, but if you bring your most important examples to lunch on Friday -- if I can help you, I'll tell you. And if I can't help you, I'll tell you that, too. Fair enough?" Here's another: "Mr. Johnson, give me a trial order and let me earn your business. If it's not everything I claim and more, you don't have to pay for it. Fair enough?" ("Fair enough" should always be accompanied by a "can't say no deal.")

And when all else fails:

7.5 Ask with humor. "Mr. Johnson, I finally figured out what it will take to get your business -- all you have to do is say yes!" The more adventurous salesperson will add -- "When would you like to do that?"

MOST IMPORTANT NOTE: Ask for the sale when the mood is right. The worst possible place is in the prospect's office. Best place is a business breakfast, lunch or dinner. Next best is your office. Next best is a trade show.

FINAL ANSWER: The key is to ask for the sale in a sincere, friendly manner. Don't push or use high pressure. The rule of thumb is: ask early, and ask often. The best way to master the skill is -- practice in front of someone who can say "Yes."

How do buyers decide, and what are buyers looking for?

Buyers are looking for 4.5 things:

1. A perceived difference in your product and service and your competitors.

2. A better perceived value in buying what you have versus buying from a competitor. Notice I did not say lower price, I said better value.

3. Little or no risk in purchasing from you. The buyer must perceive that the gain of ownership is greater than the risk of purchasing the wrong thing.

4. The buyer must like you, believe you, have confidence in you, and trust you. But it *begins* with liking you.

4.5 Lowest price. Many people (maybe even you) will think I have done them a disservice by not focusing on price concessions or winning a bid.

But, if you present the first four elements outlined above, price will go away as an issue in 60-70% of the sales you make.

FINAL ANSWER: Buyers and decision makers are looking for "comfort" not just a "deal." The decision maker has to feel that it's a good "fit" for their company, or they will pass no matter what the price. The decision maker is also going to take into account past dealings and word of mouth advertising. All buyers and decision makers in any given industry know one another. Your job, besides having a great product, is to have a great reputation. Having a great reputation reduces the perceived risk and often-times is the very key to getting the order.

PART FOUR

Sales Skill Building...
One Brick at a Time

HOW DO I BUILD
A BRICK SALES HOUSE?

ONE BRICK AT A TIME.
THE SAME WAY YOU
LEARN SALES SKILLS.

Why do buyers not return my call? How do I get my calls returned?

Should I leave a message or should I not leave a message? That's a big question isn't it? Because sometimes you leave a message (and I know this is a surprise) and they don't call you back. Rats.

That defeat tends to make you not want to leave a message more often than not. REASON: Whatever you do or whatever you want is not very important to whoever you are calling. Let me repeat that: Whatever you do or whatever you want is not very important to the person that you are calling.

What do you think keeps your customers up at night? What do you think is the biggest thing on their mind? What makes them worry? What causes their stress?

Losing or making money? That might be one. Profit? What's another one? Keeping customers loyal? Sure! What about their business? If they are in business for themselves, do you think they are concerned about making more sales of their stuff? Competition? Ouch. How about a few other concerns…

Productivity? Do you think that may be a concern of theirs? Keeping good people? Rising costs to operate? Income tax? I mean, is anybody here not concerned or angry about having to file their tax returns? Actually, I look at income taxes as rent to live in America. Makes it a lot more palatable.

Understand this: The things that keep your customers up at night have little or nothing to do with you. Your job is to try to figure out some ANSWERS to what keeps your customers up at night, and have IDEAS about what might make them sleep better. Your job is to be an *expert* at what keeps your customers up at night. And how to get them to rest peacefully.

HERE'S THE POINT: What concerns your customers and prospects is also the key to leaving a voice-mail message, and getting your call returned. Aha!

See, if you leave a bunch of puke about who you are and what you do, they don't care, and won't return your call. And there are five other guys that called them up about financial services or advertising or accounting services or copiers or cell phones (or whatever it is you sell) in the past week. And you're just one of the five. OUCH!

FINAL ANSWER: If you are going to leave message, you have to be able to give enough value or reason to get your voice mail returned. That is the whole key to response success. The answer to the question "Are you good enough to get a call returned?" depends on how much you know (or study) about how to solve or help with what concerns *them*, and leave a message about that.

Leave a message about profit, loyalty, productivity, sales, morale, family, kids – something in terms of the prospect – a tip, an idea – something that says, "I have *earned* a return call." And leave something that separates you from the other five messages about the same thing you sell.

What does the voice-mail message I leave say to my customers?

39

Pose a question and offer
an answer about them.
Or you can reverse it.
Give an answer and
pose a question.
But the key is
ABOUT THEM.

There's another strategy that is, in my opinion, the most
effective method: It is to have something of value for the
other person.

If you can generate facts about their business, their industry,
their life, their family, you leave that message, and you
dangle a carrot. Here's an example: "Mr. Johnson, there
are three things that will help you keep employees on the
job longer than anything. **Number one:** You treat your
employees better than you treat your customers. **Number
two:** You offer them benefits that help them live not die.
Number three: OOPS, I'm out of time. This is Jeffrey
Gitomer. If you want to know the third one, give me a call
at 704-333-1112." Get it? Try it.

FINAL ANSWER: You have got to have facts about them.

If you're an employment agency, they don't care about using your service, but they do care about keeping their people on the job. Now you can dangle a carrot even further. If you really want to talk to somebody, you can leave fact number one on Monday. Fact number two on Tuesday. Fact number three on Wednesday. Fact number four on Thursday. On Friday you go, "No fact today. If you want the fact, you've got to call me." Get it? Try it.

LOOK AT YOURSELF, TOO: You may also be abusing voice mail in your own business. You may not be doing it the nice way. Your customers may be calling and you may be making them angry just by the way you handle the call. You may not be there and you have a dumb voice-mail message. The voice mail works two ways. One is how you handle yours. And two is how you handle theirs. It is a given that you have to handle yours perfectly. So, focus on how you handle theirs. Get it? Try it.

I'M NOT BEGGING FOR YOUR RETURN CALL, BUT MY WIFE WILL LEAVE ME AND MY BOSS WILL KILL ME IF YOU DON'T CALL ME BACK.

What is the best way to use the Internet to make sales?

The Web is changing the sales world at net speed. How fast is net speed? One day your job is secure, next day it's obsolete. New net-sales rules? You bet.

Here are the 10.5 new reality-rules for selling at net speed:

1. The old way of selling doesn't work anymore.
Old, high-pressure, manipulative sales methods are passé. The 21st century way is creativity, value, and relationships that create a buying atmosphere, both on the 'net and in person.

2. On the Web or face-to-face, they still gotta like you.
If they like you, believe you, trust you, AND have confidence in you – then they MAY buy from you. Your job is to become likeable in person and attractive on the Web.

3. It's not just contact management anymore.
It's full contact selling. To beat the best, you gotta be one notch faster, more literate, get them information sooner, and be attractive in a daily way. Your ability to integrate computer contact, personal contact, and new economy selling skills are your keys to sales success and net mastery.

4. In sales, it's not who you know. In sales, it's who knows you.
Master the Web to create industry, market, customer, and prospect awareness. The more "value-content" in the awareness, the more attractive you become.

5. They want it now and they want it free.

You must do everything for your customers at net speed: offer information, be humanly accessible, sell what they *need* (not what you have), deliver tomorrow or sooner, respond to (and resolve) problems in an instant, inform customers how to make the best use of your product, create a problem-prevention program, and serve in a memorable way.

6. Differentiate yourself from your competition in ways other than price.

There are seven key elements in value-differentiation. Price is not one of them. Your values are: your name, your questions, your ideas, your creativity, your presentation, your perceived value, and your ability to deliver beyond the customer's expectation. If the customer or prospect perceives no "value" difference between you and your competition, they will buy price. Lowest price = lowest profit.

7. The secret to true differentiation is the Jeffrey Gitomer "value-first" proposition.

Your ability to help customers or prospects with information that will help them build their business, so that you can earn yours. "Value-first" is both the best way to differentiate *and* the highest profit maker.

8. Wow me or risk losing me.

"Satisfaction" is no longer the acceptable measure of service. Change your actions, questions, presentation, sales tools, and Web site from ordinary to extra-ordinary. Extra-ordinary leads to WOW! WOW leads to loyal -- the new measure of corporate and personal performance.

9. Study creativity to get to WOW.

Most people will agree that creativity is one of the keys to sales success in the new economy. Most people have never read a book on creativity. Read one. My favorite is *Thinkertoys* by Michael Michalko. Order it online with one-click.

10. Be accessible to the customer when THEY need you.

Understanding the customer's needs is one thing – doing something about it is another. Your highest priority is to be there when they need you and provide them with answers. The Web has changed hours of operation forever. 24.7.365 is now the minimum standard.

10.5 Most salespeople will not do the smart work and hard work it takes to make selling easy.

Yes, Dorothy, it will take hard work to gain Web mastery. It takes courage too. Invest in technology, read, compute, network, write, study, learn new, and practice. The rest is easy. The biggest key to success is to remain a student as you climb the ladder. The easiest way to get to the top is study, practice, and network your way there.

FINAL ANSWER: The Web is your new best friend and best resource. Get the best computer money will buy. Get wireless access. Get high speed at home. Get Web control of your sales life and your sales knowledge.

Master the Web and you will master your universe – and your (on-line) bank account.

Should I try to "type" the buyer?

Only if you wanna lose the sale. I believe that "typing" a buyer is a form of manipulating, if you try to modify your type with his type. Typically there are four types of people in the traditional "typing" format. In my opinion there are millions of types of people.

Personally, I don't care what type of person it is. My goal is to learn about him or her through pre-call preparation and questioning. During that time I would try to discover common ground rather than manipulative opportunities.

The object of selling is not "typing." The object of selling is engaging and harmonizing.

Some of you moan that "typing" people helps you understand them. No it doesn't. The time you spend trying to type them actually takes away from your ability to understand them.

I would much rather discover that my kid plays soccer in the same league as his kid. I would much rather find out that our favorite sports team is the same, or that we went to the same college, or that we grew up in the same neighborhood, or have a mutual friend. That's the right "type" of information.

When you're "typing," you're taking away from time that you should be harmonizing and discovering and building rapport. Spending too much time trying to figure out manipulative information about a prospect is a typographical error.

What is the best way to prepare for a sales call?

There's a 5.5 step process in preparing for a sales call, most of which can be done on your laptop computer -- hooked up to the Internet.

1. Visit the Web site of the company you are calling on.
Print out a few pages and circle areas where you have questions -- or maybe ideas. Find out everything you can about how they might use your product or service and find out everything you can about the person you are meeting with (as well as his/her boss).

2. Visit their competitor's Web site. Look for obvious differences in marketing approach or product offerings.

3. Google the name of the company you are visiting and see what comes up. Read and get further prepared.

4. Google the name of the person you are meeting with. This will reveal all kinds of personal information. If you can't find information about the person you are meeting with, you may not be meeting with the decision maker. Google the name of his boss. You may find more information there.

5. Now take all the information you have compiled and begin formulating questions based on your new knowledge of their potential need for your stuff. Try to create a couple more questions about their company and about the person if you can find their bio.

5.5 Google yourself. Never be so sales ignorant to think that the person you're meeting with for one hour isn't going to take five seconds to Google you. If you don't have a Web site, if you've never given a speech to an organization, if you've never written any articles that appeared in your trade publications, if you've never done any significant work in community or charity programs, then nothing will show up.

I've just given you the formula: make your own Web site, speak at a trade show, write articles, and involve yourself in the community. Make the person you're calling on want to meet with you. And make your research strong enough to engage the prospect in something other than product puking.

If it's a huge sale, you might want to do more personalized research -- read their annual report, call some of their customers, call some of their vendors, call their salespeople and call their PR department if they have one.

I can guarantee you one thing, whatever research you are doing now to prepare for your sales call, it's not enough. Your parents gave you this message all through out your adolescent years, "Do your homework." And all this time -- you thought it was about algebra.

BIG SECRET: They were giving you a message about life.

BIGGER SECRET: Be prepared, or be prepared to lose to someone more prepared than you are.

Should I honor a "No Soliciting" sign?

I don't. But it would depend on what it is that you're selling.

I've always looked at "solicitors" as people selling candy for phony charities, people selling perfume and art, and Fuller Brush men. (That kind of dates me, doesn't it?)

It never ceases to amaze me that businesses will go to extremes to post a no soliciting sign, instead of a welcome sign. And many businesses have a double standard in that they don't want people to solicit them, yet, they encourage their sales force to go out and cold call (AKA solicitation).

If you see a "No Soliciting" sign it's more or less words of caution. If you have something of value to sell, and a great approach, no one will perceive you as a "solicitor." Rather they'll look at you as a "professional."

FINAL ANSWER: Consider this: if they catch you soliciting -- what can they do? Call the sales police? Throw you out into the hallway? And if someone says, "Can't you read the sign on the door 'No Soliciting?'" Just respond, "Sure I could read it. I didn't think it applied to people who have something of genuine value for your business."

What is the best way to beat the competition?

All of you are hoping for some miracle answer. Well there is one. But it takes some understanding to get there. And after this short piece you still may not get it. It's subtle *and* requires more work than you're doing now. The reward is that sales will become easier to come by.

Take a look at the options for dealing with the competition and you'll get a clearer picture. You all know the options: over, under, around, and through -- well almost.

Consider these:

1. Around the competition. Getting around the competition requires connections, inside information and stealth tactics. Not to mention a bit of masterful political play. OK, OK, it's manipulative. And borders on sneaky. You have to "pull a move" to get the business. Is that bad? Depends. To get the order, no. To get future orders is where the "depends" comes in. Depending on your "around" tactics, you may have gained a poor reputation. **Be careful that your tactics don't overpower your ethics.**

2. Under the competition. Bad strategy. All bad. Undercut them by lowering your price? A one-time win where everyone loses. Low profits. Market deterioration. And the next lowest price wins the same way.

3. Through the competition. Fighting has it's place. And sometimes a fight will produce a win. Tenacity is great, but beating them down by talking trash is a losing position. Fighting them is a good philosophy. Sales is often a fight. But too often a fight for no reason. Some of the fight is based on the dreaded fear-of-loss, or desire-to-gain, rather than the less combative one preferred by the customer: desire-to-help.

HINT: You may also go "inside" the competition. Learn all you can about their strengths and weaknesses. This is especially needed for product sales.

4. Over the competition. This is the ideal way. It assumes that you take the high ground. Now don't get me wrong. It doesn't mean sit back and wait. It means rise above in a way that the competition has to respond or lose. Here are a few "over" ways. Ezine. Seminars. Referrals. Build value by building profit. Earn testimonials and use them to get over again. Others speaking on your behalf is better than any sales pitch "against" someone else. I'll make you one promise: if you invest the time and effort it takes to go "over" the competition, you will be rewarded beyond your wildest dreams, *and* sales will be easier and more fun. And once you reach a high level of "over," you will be qualified for the highest level.

4.5 Ignore the competition. I have spent the last ten years going "over" the competition. Building my own skills and writing. They keep reading my weekly article in their hometown. Do I know them? Some. Most I don't. Sales and competition share the same adage. "It's not who you know, it's who knows you." Sounds a bit stuffy, but let me assure you that it's better to build your skills than to try and "beat" someone. I go for "best" not "beat." It's a better, cleaner win.

Do I always win? No, but I always feel I should have.
I have a self-confidence that keeps me ready for the next
opportunity. And I wake up the next day and go to work
sharpening my skills.

EPILOG: I'm not giving you a simple solution as I usually do.
Rather I'm presenting facts and philosophy and letting you
make your own decisions about how you want to "handle"
the competition. Some of you reading this will think that my
way is foolish, idealistic, or worse -- not do-able. That will
only help the people you hate. The competition.

My ways of dealing
with my competition
(over or ignore)
are the hardest ways –
but they work.
And the longer you
go over them, the more
you can ignore them.

What is the best way to ensure I get a reorder?

From the moment you get the first order from any customer, your report card begins. And the cool part is, you choose your own grade.

The next order will depend on the "yes factor" of the following 6.5 key elements:

1. Was your product delivered on time?

2. Were all your promises kept?

3. Were service issues resolved favorably?

4. Did you follow up after the service?

5. Is it easy to find anyone in your company (at any time)?

6. Did you stay in contact with them on a regular basis in between sales with some kind of message of value?

6.5 How accessible and responsive are you?

THINK ABOUT THIS: Customers vote with their money and view your performance from the last encounter to the moment they need you again. If they bought from you before, half the battle is won. The reorder is a report card on what happened in that time. When an existing customer says, "Jump," how fast you are able to say, "How high?" will determine your fate. It's easier than shopping around.

FINAL NOTE: If they come back asking for a price concession, the likelihood that you will have to give it will be in inverse proportion to the quality of service they have received between orders.

What is the best way to follow-up?

One word: Creatively.

Two words: With Value.

Three words: Gain their interest.

Four words: Nothing about your wallet.

Five words: Something different than the competition.

Six words: Offer something to advance the sale.

Seven words: Tell them you have a new idea.

Eight words: Tell them to expect a package tomorrow morning.

Nine words: Make a firm appointment before you leave their office.

Nine.five words: Don't do anything that makes you look like a jack-ass.

The key to follow-up is being smart and creative.

Smart is never sending a proposal without making a firm follow-up appointment either in person or on the phone. Something written down and agreed to. Something that leads you closer to the sale. Something that proves they're interested in buying from you. Make that appointment, and you become an elite salesperson, because most salespeople (you included) send a proposal and then begin a follow-up process that's somewhere between lame and laughable.

Creative is doing something that gains the attention of the buyer and forces a positive response.

I have a customer who is a dedicated father and grandfather. He loves his children. He *really* loves his grandchildren. How did I find this out? One day we started talking about family. Turns out, we both have three daughters and three granddaughters. Common ground? You bet! At a bookstore in New York City, I picked up a few children's books, signed by the author, that had won awards for both design and readability. (He loves to read to his grandchildren.) I gave him one book for each grandchild. Without going into detail, I can tell you that a traditional, corporate gift could not have meant more, or created a deeper emotional response. Did it help our relationship? You bet it did! But, I gave the same gift to myself -- so I could read to my grandchildren.

PLEASE NOTE: I didn't give this gift to make a sale. He was already my customer. I gave this gift to further our friendship. Follow-up is not just about selling. Follow-up is about surprising, caring, paying attention, and thinking about others in the same way that you think about yourself. It's about walking the same talk you're talking.

What are the best ways to add value?

This is a trick question. Every company in the world tries to create some half-baked "value added" program that no salesperson can ever explain. It's a bunch of stuff from the company that "adds" on to a sale, but has nothing to do with the customer (let alone give them value).

If you're trying to earn an order, *adding value* is a bit too late. It may be a weak incentive, but if you're up against me, you're going to lose. My philosophy has always been, create enough value to trigger the law of attraction (they call me, not me call them). Added value means you gotta "sell" it. I want people to buy.

In order for people to *buy*, you have to re-look at how you address the value you seek to add, and you have to reposition the way you offer it. Look at these value structures and tell me how they compare to "value-added."

Here are some real value words that put "added value" where it belongs -- out of the business and sales lexicon:

☆ **Bring value**
☆ **Be of value**
☆ **Instill value**
☆ **Offer value**
☆ **Value provider**
☆ **Give value first**

What is "give value first?"

Value first means they have bought it. I want to be on the buy side.

Since March 23, 1992, I have understood and benefited from the concept of *giving value first*.

That's the day my first column appeared in the *Charlotte Business Journal*. Since that day, I have booked more than 1500 seminars, sold 750,000 books, collected millions of dollars in revenues, and I've become one of the best known salespeople in the world without making one sales call, thus proving my #1 rule of sales: **People don't like to be sold, but they love to buy**.

Thousands of people come to my Web site every day. One hundred thousand read my free weekly ezine (*Sales Caffeine*), and millions of people read my column each week that appears in 100 business papers around the United States.

All I do is share a little of my sales knowledge, share a little of my sales wisdom, share a few of my sales ideas, for free.

And all that happens is my phone rings off the hook. The marketing strategy I use is one that appears in no textbook in the world. Yet, I would challenge any marketing genius who tells me that an ad is better than a column in the paper to get notoriety and response. I can get one hundred times greater response with my method than they can with theirs, and at least one thousand times greater quality of lead. The people who read my stuff (you included) are willing to spend money to get more of my stuff.

My multi-million dollar value marketing strategy is:

I put myself in front of people who can say yes to me, and I deliver value first.

One of the main reasons that you'll never see a "value first" campaign run by any marketing firm or advertising agency is because they don't make any percentages giving things away for free. Personally, I'm in favor of their strategy because it allows me to make millions of dollars as long as they continue to do it. If they ever started doing it my way, I would actually have competition. At the moment, I just look at what they do and laugh. I laugh when I see it, I laugh as I watch my phone ring, and I laugh hardest on my way to the bank.

ACTION: Start collecting e-mail addresses. Start your weekly e-mail magazine next week. Start writing articles in front of your customers who will then perceive you as an expert, not a salesperson. Start speaking at trade shows instead of just attending them. Giving value first is not an option if you seek to be a sales winner. This page contains more than an answer. It contains a philosophy and a success strategy for life.

49

How can I create
more valuable questions?

> By knowing about things that your
> customer considers valuable,
> and creating questions that makes
> the customer think about themselves
> and respond in terms of you.

For example, you're a retail-clothing salesman, a customer walks in your store, you ask, "When someone looks at what you're wearing, what do you want them to think?" They answer, and you follow with, "What are they thinking now?" The customer may say something, but they'll be low key. And you end with, "Would you be open to trying on a few pieces that I believe will give you the look you're trying to achieve?"

Those questions beat, "Can I help you?" It also engages the customer in what may be most valuable to them: their image.

Here's another example. Let's say you're selling real estate, and you're taking a family out to look at homes. You ask the woman, "When you're looking out the kitchen window, what do you want to see?" This question gets at the heart of her emotion.

You could have asked something dumb, like, "How much were you looking to spend on a home?" I consider that question a violation of their personal information, and none of your business -- unless they want to volunteer it.

FINAL ANSWER: In order to create a valuable question, you have to learn what will strike importance or emotion in the mind of the prospect or the customer. The key is to ask a question that has nothing to do with your sale or your money. Questions about money have been misnamed "qualifying questions." They should be named "privacy violations."

HERE'S THE FORMULA: The more valuable information you gather, the more you will be able to create valuable questions. The more proficient you become at asking valuable questions -- the more valuable your bank account will become.

HERE'S A VALUABLE QUESTION: CAN WE HAVE DINNER SATURDAY NIGHT?

HERE'S MY FINAL ANSWER: NO.

What is the "sale after the sale?"

When you've made a delivery, that's when you begin to build the relationship for the next sale.

Combine this answer with "What's the best way to ensure I get a reorder?" (question 45) and you'll begin to understand what a loyal customer is.

The biggest corporate failure in America (yes, even bigger than their illegal accounting practices) is their ineptitude in communicating with their existing customer base with anything other than a sales message.

If you're looking for the sale after the sale, there has to be a continuum, a weekly continuum of value messages, so that you are proving your worth, and building your goodwill, week after week -- after consistent week.

You're also keeping your name and your company's name at the top of their mind. I refer to it as top of mind awareness, but I would imagine others do as well. This top of mind awareness, when linked to the perceived value of their relationship with you, ensures the fact that the next time they need your product or service they're going to call you first.

FINAL ANSWER: The sale after the sale is *not* the reorder. The sale after the sale are the actions that you take to ensure the fact that the reorder is yours.

Why do customers cancel?

Buyer's remorse is one of the biggest, unspoken dilemmas in sales.

You get a big order. Two days later you get an e-mail or a fax -- never a phone call -- telling you to cancel the order. Or worse, you call the customer to confirm, and somehow they evaporate from the face of the earth.

This especially happens on big ticket items like cars, houses, pianos, or boats. Items bought emotionally, and when they went home and thought about it, decided they couldn't afford it. (Or decided they didn't really want it, or were influenced by other people not to do it, or got into an argument with their spouse about it.)

Even the government knows that people have buyers remorse. That's why the law was passed to allow people to change their minds without penalty and a three-day cancel clause was put into all retail accounts.

Some salespeople are foolish enough to use this as a selling feature when, in fact, they're putting cancellation in the mind of the customer. What they need to do, is reinforce the positive elements, and prepare the customer for the fact that they may have seconds thoughts, and what to do about them.

The reason you don't do this is that you were too chicken to tell the customer what to do in case they had a change of heart.

Here's what to do: Tell the customer that when they get home, they may begin to think about affordability, or think they could of gotten it someplace cheaper, or be influenced by others. And you tell them what to do in each case. You can even give them a sheet of paper to reinforce their ideas. Or maybe even a CD-ROM with a brief video you made about why people cancel for the wrong reasons.

SECRET:

The secret is to remind them why they bought in the first place.

Reinforce their reasons for buying without using any sales techniques. Make certain that you have covered their logical and emotional reasons for buying. If you only do logic, or you only do emotion -- it's more likely you will lose the sale.

What is the best way to get out of a slump?

Let me ask you these 4.5 questions:

1. **What market conditions have changed over the last six months?**

2. **What competitive conditions have changed over the last six months?**

3. **Why did you lose your last five sales? (The real reason, not just lowest price.)**

4. **Are you working as hard as you did your first month on the job?**

4.5 **What are you doing with your spare hours to help yourself get better?**

Most salespeople who get into a slump are there because of something they did, and they're not really working hard enough to get out of it. Oh, they're pressing for the sale, but they're not trying to cure their slump.

Some salespeople blame it on bad luck. My mentors taught me hard work makes luck.

Examine the little things first. Your work habits. Your persistence. Your existing attitude versus your attitude when you're winning. Your ability to get calls returned. Your ability to get face to face meetings. And especially what you're doing after work.

Now let's take a look at the big picture.

When a ballplayer or a golfer has a slump, they take extra coaching, and they practice extra hard. Is that what you're doing?

FINAL ANSWER: If you discover why your slump is occurring, that's the first step to real recovery. The second step is to keep your attitude higher than it's ever been before. But you can shorten a slump by tapping into the "Yes" side of your brain and leaving "No" where it belongs -- in the gutter with the other losers.

Believe you will, and act as if it's happened.

Read more about being in a slump in my other book, The Little Red Book of Selling, *pages 38-42.*

What are the biggest mistakes salespeople make?

1. Getting into sales for the money. If you don't love what you do, you will never achieve the goals that you've set for yourself, let alone the arbitrary ones your company sets for you (also known as quotas). If you're in sales for the money, get out now and become a lawyer, or worse, a politician.

2. Failure to realize that their attitude is at the core of their success. A big part of selling is thinking that you can, and a positive anticipation of going into a sales meeting. A big part of selling is expecting a positive outcome. You can't do any of these without a positive attitude *before* you start.

3. Blaming other people instead of taking responsibility. It's real easy for everyone else to be at fault when something goes wrong. People not showing up for work. People not keeping their promises. People not delivering the goods. Or people not doing their homework. Major clue: If you are relying on other people to help make your sale, then you are completely responsible to follow up with them in advance to make certain that they have done their part. Most failures are based on poor communication rather than poor execution.

4. Blaming other circumstances instead of taking responsibility. Our computers are down. Our phones are down. The truck broke down. FedEx didn't make it. Why don't you just tell me the dog ate your homework? Just go back to the third grade where you made excuses that were equally as silly. But in the third grade it didn't matter. Blaming outcomes on "things" only makes you look like an incompetent twit. You're better off with a response that starts out, "You're in luck. FedEx didn't deliver the part, so I went to our competitor, bought you what you needed, and am personally going to bring it by this morning so you can have it on time." WOW!

5. Trying to sell instead of getting people to buy. Too many salespeople have to explain who they are and what they do. Failing to realize that the prospective customer has heard the same pitch 20 times. From my perspective, a sales interview (erroneously known as a sales presentation) should consist of 75% questions. The answers derived from those questions will let the customer and the probable purchaser prove to him or herself the degree of their need, the experiences they've had up until now, why you are the best choice, and how they can buy now.

5.5 Not having a deep enough belief in what it is you are selling. It blows me away how few salespeople believe in their own product or service. At a 6 a.m. sales training meeting for a car dealership, I asked 30 salespeople how many of them drove the brand of car that they sold. Half of the room raised their hand. I asked the other half to leave because there was no way they could sell something they didn't believe in enough to own. If you don't own what you're selling, go sell something else.

Salespeople make tons of mistakes. I could talk about giving their price too soon, following up incorrectly, trying to use time worn sales techniques, or not being friendly enough. But if you take the above 5.5 answers to heart, it will lead you to more sales than you can imagine. Those sales will turn into relationships if your belief is deep enough.

What are the fatal flaws of selling?

In 25 years (has it been that long?) of sales training, I've never had a salesperson come up to me and say, "Jeffrey, I didn't make the sale and it was all my fault."

Salespeople make the fatal mistake of blaming other things, circumstances, and people for their own inability to create a buying atmosphere. And that mistake has double jeopardy: One, you're blaming the wrong party, and two, because you issue blame instead of taking responsibility. You fail to see the urgent need for more self-improvement training.

I have identified 12.5 fatal flaws of selling, the real reasons why salespeople fail to make the sale. Five are here, the other 7.5 are on my Web site. If you like the first five, and you don't go to the Web site to get the other 7.5, that would be your first fatal flaw. Painful as this exercise may be, why don't you rate yourself instead of just reading them.

And for your maximum enjoyment and benefit, a one sentence "flawless" remedy or suggestion follows each flaw. *Please* re-read it several times – until you admit that it's you, not them.

How many of these are fatal to you? Go get a **red** pen and as you read, put an "**F**" by the flaws you may want to improve.

1. Being a puppy, puppet or pawn. "Send me a brochure!" "Send me a proposal!" "OK! I'll do it." Salespeople are too happy to oblige without getting a commitment or adding an idea. **Flawless:** When you send a brochure, make an appointment at the same time. When you get a request for a proposal, change some of the terms to favor your selection.

2. Speaking before asking. Does a doctor tell you where he went to medical school? No. How many years he's been practicing? No. He asks, "Where does it hurt?" **Flawless:** Ask compelling questions. Ask questions that reveal pain or emotion. Ask questions your competition doesn't ask.

3. Making a verbal agreement for services to be provided. Nothing is more fatal than a prospect thinking there is more to the deal than you do. When the prospect says. "I thought you said…" whatever follows is a problem. **Flawless:** Write down and repeat back ALL promises and terms.

4. Negatively referring to the competition. OK, they're a bunch of dirty rotten creeps. What's your point? When you put them down, you degrade yourself. **Flawless:** Always refer to the competition as "industry standard," and "my worthy competition."

5. Following up to see if you "got my literature," and to see if you "have any questions." The salesman thinks he is being seen as helpful and professional – actually he is a pest and looks dumb. **Flawless:** Call with ideas and smart questions.

Free Red Bit:

For the other 7.5, just go to www.gitomer.com, register if you are a first time user, and enter the words FATAL FLAWS in the RedBit box.

What should a business lunch consist of?

There are 4.5 business lunch categories:

1. Building a relationship and trying to make connections.

2. New prospective customer not looking to buy yet.

3. New prospective customer getting ready to buy.

4. Existing customer who you are building a relationship with and/or who is ready to buy.

4.5 GREAT food.

Lunch should consist of at least 1/3 relationship building talk. Talk about things you have in common (golf, sports, college, home state) as much as you can. Talk about customers in common or business things you have in common (experiences, jobs, etc). Talk about your specific agenda. If you don't have time for business talk, it was a very successful lunch. That means you talked about things in common and had a great time.

HERE'S AN IDEA: The four-way lunch. Get your customer to bring a referral for you, and you bring a referral for your customer. Your customer may be reluctant to bring you a referral *unless* you bring one for him. Think about how powerful this scenario is, then try it one or two times.

Should I golf for business? How?

Ask *any* salesperson where he or she would rather sell --
an office or a golf course. Golf course wins 99-1. Hole-in-
one, baby! Then ask them if they know the best time to ask
for an order, and they will all get a double bogey.

Even though you have your golf clothes on, your personality
is bare. It's not a matter of you selling the customer, it's a
matter of the customer buying you. If you are looking to sell
something on the golf course, sell yourself.

Here are the factors your customer or prospect learns about
you during a round of golf: Can I play with this person? Can
I tolerate this person? Mutual compatibility – do I like this
person? Do I believe this person? Do I have anything in
common with this person? What is the personality of this
person? What are the ethics of this person? How much is this
person paying attention?

The important thing to realize is that both parties playing golf
are judging each other. Your temperament, ethics, and manners
are also on display. Your language, your drinking, your ability
to follow the rules, and your sportsmanship are determining
factors in your ability to build a relationship and get the
business.

HERE'S WHAT TO DO: Meet on the practice tee an hour before
tee-off time. Bring fruit, muffins, coffee, orange juice, minor
nourishment to get rolling. Warm up for at least 30 minutes

by hitting a bucket of balls with your prospect and getting to know him or her a little better. Then move to the practice green. Hit a few balls out of the sand. Sink a few putts. Now you're warm and so is your prospect. Now you're ready to go to the first tee.

Select strategic people to play with your prospect. The best person is a prospect for him or her. That way everyone can do business on the golf course. A foursome is not mandatory.

Make the round relaxing. On the first tee, I like to give everyone a couple of sleeves of the best balls on the market. It's a surprise, and it sets the tone. Make sure your golf cart is loaded with the prospect's favorite food and drinks based on your conversation with an administrative person.

Play the first nine holes, and only talk about golf. It's what you have in common. The best round you've ever played, the best shots you've ever made, you know, golf-talk.

I refer to the back nine as the business nine. If you've gained enough rapport on the front nine, business should be an easy subject on the back nine.

CAUTION: The person you're playing with will never remember the score. BUT, they will ALWAYS remember that you cheated on the third hole.

FINAL ANSWER: The key is to make certain that you show your best side, your honest side, your ethical side, your service side, your friendship side, and your fun side. All of these will be business-building elements on the golf course -- as long as you don't show your back side.

What should I say when the customer calls and he's mad as hell?

Anything except, "I'm sorry!"

You can say, "I apologize," but that's not what the customer is looking for. You can begin to tell your story about what happened, but that's not what the customer is looking for. You can try to blame some thing, or someone else, for what went wrong, but that's not what the customer is looking for.

> The customer is looking
> for two things. They want
> to know that you care about
> them personally, and they
> want to know what you are
> going to do about it now.

The best way to apologize is to let the customer vent first. Don't interrupt, just take notes and make empathetic noises. You can even tell the customer that it makes you mad too. Second, ask the customer what their speed of need is. Do they need it by tomorrow? Do they need it today? Or did they need it yesterday?

Most customers will have needed it yesterday. This is your big chance to be memorable, by getting it there the day before yesterday (just kidding). The reality is, their need for speed will determine your action plan for recovery. Realize that you have hit a flash-point and are in jeopardy of losing the customer. Therefore, any action you take towards recovery is a positive one.

The interesting news is that most big companies have firm policies in place that preclude memorable recovery: needing an invoice, needing a customer number, needing a return shipment authorization, and other crapola that *no* angry customer wants to hear.

FINAL ANSWER: Tell them what they want to hear. That you apologize, that you understand how they feel, that you are meeting with the appropriate people to get a resolve, and that it will be done in 24-hours. No blame, no excuses, no drama.

EPILOG: Follow up with a personal call, and a personal note of thanks. This makes the recovery complete, and paves the way for the next order, or a favorable referral.

I LOVE WHEN PEOPLE
SWEAR AT ME. IT
MEANS WE SCREWED
UP, AND NOW I HAVE A
CHANCE TO RECOVER!

How can I prevent the prospect from going with the lowest price?

I wish I had a dollar for every salesperson who told me the biggest objection he or she gets is "price." Price is a complex objection (I refer to it as a barrier) that deals with customer sub-headings like -- real need, affordability, hidden agendas, value, prospect perception, prospect untruths, combined with your communication, validation, differentiation, and valuation by the salesperson. The only good news about price objections is that they are often buying signals in disguise.

A major part of the price problem is that many salespeople believe that they (or their company) are the same or worse than their competition. Fortunately, there are two quick fixes for this situation -- change your belief, or change your employer.

Six things you can do to keep price integrity:

1. Support the price you give as the true price. "Let me tell you why…"

2. Use the fact of higher price as the reason to buy. "You get the highest level of service after the sale…"

3. Use testimonials. "Here are three video testimonials from others who have paid our price and loved it…"

4. Sell your competitive edge, not your price. "We're the company who holds the patent…"

5. Sell the decision maker on the relationship. "In order to serve you after the sale in the manner you expect…"

6. Sell everything *but* price. Start with quality, value and overall cost. If you're not the lowest price -- be the best value, have the lowest overall cost and the finest product, have the highest productivity and the fastest (legendary) service.

Statistics show 74% of price cuts are started by salespeople -- not customers. And most price resistance comes from salespeople, not buyers. The salesperson already knows everyone's price and will immediately begin to compensate for it in the sales presentation. In their own mind, they believe the customer always goes for the lowest price. Big mistake.

TRY THIS TACTIC: If you have to submit bids, change the rules. Ask the DECISION MAKER (this may not be the person you're talking to) to consider taking BEST, not PRICE. Ask, "If all the bids are within 10% of one another, would you consider dropping lowest price and selecting who you think would be the best? Best people to work with, best product, and best service."

Now, they won't always say "Yes," but what do you have to lose by asking?

TRY THIS TACTIC: Make testimonials an integral part of the proposal or bid. Tell the buyer that all the people he's considering are just telling him they're the best. Why not make them prove it instead of just bragging about it. Put a clause in the bid requirements that all claims for product and service must be supported by an existing customer (third party) video testimonial.

Now, they won't always say "yes," but what do you have to lose by making the suggestion?

Price issues compel salespeople to be their creative best.

Price issues compel salespeople to believe their product or service is the best.

Price issues compel salespeople to use customer's testimonials to help make the sale.

FINAL THOUGHT: To understand price, you have to come to the realization that it's not just the relationship, or your product, it's *their* money. And they won't let go of the wallet until they feel comfortable, perceive a greater value, and have little or no risk. They're going to guard their dollars, just like you do. But, you don't always buy the lowest price, and neither will they.

How can I make my proposal stand out?

By putting an executive summary on the front page of it, so no one has to read the boring thing unless they want to.

One of the main reasons proposals exist is because buyers think they can get the lowest price (or the best deal) by pitting one company against the other.

The key is to make yourself the winner *before* the proposal happens.

You do this by creating conditions, or terms, that preclude others from either bidding or winning.

HERE'S A STRATEGY: Just say "No" when they ask for a proposal. When someone asks me for a proposal, the first thing I say to them is, "No." That always shocks people. And besides, proposals are a pain in the butt.

I ask the person if they were taking notes. They say, "Yes." I say, "Well, let me just sign the notes." I continue by saying, "All we really need to do is pick a date to begin." And 30% of the time the prospect will say, "You're right."

The other 70% of the time the prospect will insist on a proposal. But I've just won 30% of the business without submitting a piece of paper. And there's a reason for this. I have sales guts, and you don't.

Proposals are there to lower risk to the buyer, and potentially to lower the cost.

But in the final analysis, many proposals can be eliminated if your prospect feels that your price is fair, and that their risk is low. If the risk is low, and the reward is high, then the answer is always obvious: YOU WIN!

FINAL ANSWER: Effective proposals are a result of effective sales presentations. Proposals should be the solidifying factor, not the sales pitch. The proposal should document what has been said and agreed upon. The proposal should confirm the sale and all the claims you made about it.

Does yours?

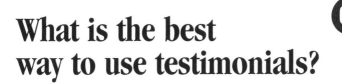

What is the best way to use testimonials?

60

The absolute best way to use a testimonial is in video format at the end of a sale as proof to the customer that you are who you say you are, that your product does what you said it would do, that your service or services are the best on the planet, and that your price is both fair and of fair value.

That's the simple answer. If you become a testimonial-based seller, (which I believe to be the most powerful form of sales in the world), then you can get testimonials for every element, or every step, of your sales cycle.

For example, if you have a customer who will not give you an appointment, send them a CD of one of your customers that says, "For two years I would not give this guy an appointment. It was one of the biggest mistakes I ever made in business. If Bill calls you, invite him into your office and let him do for you what he did for me." If you can't get an appointment after that, you suck.

You can use testimonials to answer questions. You can use testimonials to overcome a price objection. You can use testimonials to overcome, "I'm satisfied with my present supplier." You can use testimonials to affirm all the promises or claims that you make.

FINAL ANSWER: Throw away your testimonial letters that relate to sales, and use video-based words of support and proof from the customers who love you the most.

What do I say to my customer when my competition lies about me, my product, or my company?

Take the high road, and don't try to rectify or justify what was said.

Rather say, "We can't be responsible for other people's irresponsibility. Our responsibility comes from our years of delivering quality, delivering on time, servicing memorably, and creating a valuable partnership between ourselves and our customers."

"Mr. Prospect, I have found the best way for a prospective customer like yourself to discover the truth! And, so there's no short-term or long-term confusion, you should require video testimonials from existing loyal customers for all claims made by either me or my worthy competitor. I think it would also be important that you require all potential vendors to provide two testimonials from companies that used to use us, but switched, and two testimonials from companies that used to use our competition, and switched to us. I can provide those testimonials to you tomorrow. It will be interesting to see what my competitor has to say about doing the same thing."

GOOD NEWS: Without you having to respond to their lies directly, this will kick your competition's ass into the dirt.

NOTE TO ALL SALESPEOPLE: If you do not have an arsenal of video testimonials that support your claims, overcome all customer objections, and talk about using your biggest competitor and then switching to you, you're operating at an extreme disadvantage.

Make arrangements to gather testimonial videos that provide proof and overcome objections as fast as you can.

FINAL ANSWER: Salespeople feel they have to defend their honor in order to "combat" the competition's lies. Wrong. The best defense is a great offense. The cool part about the strategy outlined above is that it can be used in every sale you make, whether the competition lies about you or not.

How do I beat "Call Reluctance?"

Reluctance is a form of fear. Fear of the unknown, fear of rejection, fear of failing.

Call Reluctance is a mental disease of salespeople that leads to excuses -- both to oneself and to others (mostly bosses). Excuses make me puke.

You justify your reasons for not calling new prospects because:

☎ You're too busy!

☎ You have existing clients who need your help.

☎ You haven't mastered your new product information.

☎ The educational classes your company offers are too good to resist.

☎ It's too near the holiday or it's just after the holiday.

☎ It's too early. It's too late. It's too hot. It's too cold. In short, any excuse you can create.

THOUGHT:

If you're scared to make sales calls, get out of sales.

Call Reluctance is NOT A PROBLEM, it's a symptom. If you want to get over it, find out what's causing it (the *real* problem), and you will be the winner in the battle for who (or what) controls your mind. And your bank account.

FINAL ANSWER: If you feel Call Reluctance creeping in, start the turnaround process right away. Believe in yourself. Inspire yourself to take action. Review past victories to give present self-confidence, and ensure future success by visualizing the success that will come.

Now, pick your butt up and make a few calls.

What kind of thank you note should I write?

One that says "thank you," cites something personal, and leaves the receiver looking forward to more.

The shorter it is -- the better it is.
The more handwritten it is --- the better it is.
The more personalized it is -- the better it is.
The more sincere it is -- the better it is.

Here's an example:

Dear Josh,

Thanks for your business. I've had a great time getting to know you.

I am looking forward to getting together with you for a Bobcats game when the season begins. Since we both went to Ohio State, it will be interesting to watch Steve Smith play. It's almost like having two teams to cheer for.

I will stay in close contact as we make our first delivery, and set our relationship in motion.

Feel free to call me at any time. (Except during working hours, after work, or on the weekends -- oh, and not on holidays either!)

Best Regards,
Jeffrey Gitomer
555-555-5555 -- personal cell

Notice I didn't repeat anything.

Notice I didn't say "Again, thanks."
Once is enough.

Notice I told him two times that
I would be connecting with him soon.

Notice I reassured him that
I would be there through the delivery
and setting up process.

Notice I made it funny.

Notice I made it personal.

Notice I gave him my cell number.

How excellent are my selling skills?

What's the biggest sale you've ever made? How many big sales have you made? How many unsolicited referrals do you get? How often do people return your calls? Every action a customer takes is a report card on your skills. You're probably not that good, even though you think you are.

Here's how to become a great salesperson – even if you think you already are.

Question one: Think you're pretty good at sales? Sure you do. Making a good living – at the top of your game or team. Driving the new car, got the perks, and business is good.

Question two: Any room for improvement? Sure there is. More than you think.

Question three: Got a game plan to double your sales skills and sales revenue this year? Ouch.

Don't feel too bad, most people don't. Most don't believe doubling is even possible. These people are in the category of "too smart." They already know all the answers. And even if you're good, someone else is better. Your biggest hope is that they don't work for your competition.

"OK, Jeffrey, get to the point. How do I get "way" better? How do I double?" you ask (hoping for the two sentence panacea).

I'll give it to you in one sentence: **Get every customer you have to bring you one new customer just like them.** There it is. Assuming you maintain your level of business with existing customers, your business will double.

But that's just an answer. Pay attention here and I'll give you the game plan. That's what you really want: the proven formula. The how-to.

"Sounds like work, Jeffrey," you begin to moan.

"You bet, baby," says I. "BUT – I guarantee that you will beat your competition, AND earn more than you have ever earned before – as long as you're willing to learn (and try) as you've never learned before, and work a little harder than you're working now. Learning, trying new, hard work, and earning go hand-in-hand. Or should I say hand-in-wallet."

And let me be clear. There are no sales techniques in this formula. This is not how-to-sell per-se. This is how to succeed. If you learn how to succeed, selling becomes *much* easier.

How to succeed will help formulate and clarify your philosophy and strategy of selling. Once you realize that you "sell to help" instead of "selling to total up your commissions," you'll need a calculator with more zeroes.

Wanna measure your selling skills? There are skill assessments you can take. Go to www.trainone.com and click on our sample sales assessment. But, the real test of your sales prowess can be measured by the number of customers who stay with you, buy again, and refer you to others.

THE ACTION-FORMULA. Here are the 10.5 action elements that will take your selling skills from good to great – then from great to greatest:

1. Read about positive attitude 15 minutes a day. Two pages a day from Carnegie, Hill, or Peale. Your attitude determines everything you do. If you don't start there, you can never get anywhere. (Quick self test: If you're constantly blaming other things and people for your failings, it's your negative attitude that's in the way.)

2. Read one sales book a quarter. Reading helps you expose yourself to new sales information. Look at my Web site (www.gitomer.com) for a complete list.

3. Read one personal development book a quarter.
Rather than just work on sales techniques, work on yourself. Health habits, personal skills, personal growth, and life understanding. Best books: *Think and Grow Rich* by Napoleon Hill, and *How to Win Friends and Influence People* by Dale Carnegie.

4. Read one creativity book a year. Salespeople differentiate themselves with creativity and enthusiasm. They create attraction by being different. This is a learned skill. Best book: *Thinkertoys* by Michael Michalko.

5. Attend 4 sales seminars a year. Invest in self-learning. Learn new things and meet other learners.

6. Listen to sales CDs and tapes twice as much as you listen to radio in the car. Repetition is one of the keys to mastery. The other is practice what you learn as soon as you learn it.

7. Record yourself reading a book on sales. By recording a book yourself, you will master the sales skills *and* hear your presentation skills at the same time. It is a powerful exercise. Read and record 30-minutes a week.

8. Post your goals in front of your face and say them twice a day. I post my goals on my bathroom mirror to remind myself as I start my thinking for the day. SECRET: When I achieve one of my goals I take it off my bathroom mirror and re-post it on my bedroom mirror, so that each morning as I dress I can see my success. Goals are your roadmap.

9. Have real sales training for 30-minutes a week in sales meetings with your friends or co-workers. Weekly meetings and sales training helps you build your knowledge in a real learning environment. Give yourself the gift of new knowledge, strategy reinforcement, and inspirational material you can use the minute you leave the meeting.

10. Record yourself making a sales presentation. THE MOST IMPORTANT PART OF THE FORMULA. If you do all the other parts of the formula, and never hear how you sell, you'll never improve. The day you hear yourself trying to make a sale, is the FIRST DAY of your success quest. Caution: It's as painful as it is powerful.

10.5 Tear out this list. Study it, copy it, post it in several places, and turn each action-element into a goal. Make it part of your being for one year and it will become part of your life forever.

What is the best way to make my quota every month?

Figure out a way to make it in your first week instead of your last week.

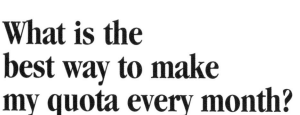

Quotas are arbitrary, stupid numbers mostly set by people who can't make sales. People who concentrate predominantly on "numbers."

Most salespeople who can't make quota either lack selling skills or a deep belief in what they sell. If this is you, get more skills or change jobs.

If you're struggling to make quota consider this: Suppose your quota were double and you had to make 25% of your quota each week instead of your whole quota on the last day of the month (which is what you're doing now). Could you do it?

Answer: Sure you can. On one condition. Your pipeline has to have enough prospective sales in there to make that happen. Let's say your quota is $50,000 a month in sales ($12,500 a week), your commission rate is 10% and your closing ratio is 25%. In order to make your $50,000 quota in a month, you must have $200,000 worth of sales in your pipeline (or at least $50,000 in any given week).

Let's break it down further. Let's say it takes you three calls to get one appointment. So if it takes you 4 appointments to get one sale -- it will take you 12 calls to get one sale. See how easy it is once you break the numbers down? If you're not lying about your numbers, then making your quota is only a matter of filling your pipeline by working your own numbers.

FINAL ANSWER: Most salespeople don't make quota because they don't have enough in their pipeline, and the reason you don't have enough in your pipeline is because you're not working hard enough to fill it. If it doesn't go into the pipe, it's never going to come out of the pipe. That's why they call it a pipeline.

What is the best way to manage my time?

Take control of it.

Everyone says they have "no time." That's baloney – everyone has the same amount of time, it just depends whether you spend it or invest it.

Spending time is watching TV. Investing time is reading a book that will help you get better. Most people spend their time, when they should be investing it.

FINAL ANSWER:

If you're doing the right thing with your time, you're investing it.

Wherever you are, whatever you're doing, the time is always the same.

The time is now.

Why do I quit so easy when the customer tells me, "No?" How long should I have hung in there?

67

Salespeople hate rejection. So much so that they're only willing to take it once per sale. As soon as the customer says, "I'm not interested," the salesperson quits. As soon as the customer says, "We're satisfied with who we're doing business with," the salesperson quits.

ANSWER: One of the main reasons that you quit so easily is that your belief system is limited or weak. You lack the passion that it takes to hang in there and win the order.

How many "No's" are YOU willing to take before you give up on the sale? There's an old adage that says, "Most sales are made after the seventh NO." That doesn't mean the customer has told you "No" seven times. What it means is that they've put up seven barriers. And you've been able to hang in until the end -- to win the order. It means when someone says, "We're not interested," you dig in deeper and harder -- asking more questions, and becoming more interesting.

Two of the questions I'm asked most is, "Jeffrey, when do I give up on a customer?" and "When do I throw in the towel?" My answer is simple:

When you believe in your heart that you can no longer help that customer, or that your solution is not the best for that customer, then you quit, but UNTIL then, you hang in there until they say "No" ten times (maybe eleven).

SECRET: Rephrase my answer above and deliver it to the customer as follows: "Mr. Jones, I must be doing something wrong because you continue to reject me. In my heart I believe that we're the best value and the best answer for your needs. And until we are able to do business together, I'm hanging in there. With your permission, I will continue to follow-up with you until you scream at me to go away, or you simply throw me out a window. Is that fair enough?"

The customer will smile and be impressed about your deep belief and commitment, and may even place an order.

What is the best way to ⑥⑧ double my sales this year?

There are only 2.5 ways of doubling your existing sales income:

1. Double the amount of people who you sit in front of that can say "Yes" to you.

2. Get every customer you have this year to stay with you, and bring you one new customer just like them next year.

2.5 A combination of answers one and two. But this requires the two word secret ingredient: HARD WORK.

Salespeople spend hundreds of hours doing non-sales things and only minutes in front of decision makers. Reverse this and your sales won't double, they'll triple. Hundreds of thousands of salespeople will double their sales and/or double their income this year. The only question is, will one of them be you?

FINAL THOUGHT: Stop thinking small. Stop thinking quota. Stop thinking end of the month. Start making better use of your sales time. Start making bigger sales. Start now.

Who is the most important person in the world?

If you're asking that question to me, the answer is easy: Me. If I ask the question of you, you might hesitate.

If I rephrase the question and say, "When you're speaking with your biggest customer, who's the most important person in the world?" The answer is still you, even though you think it might be the customer. The object of sales and the object of life are the same: be the best person you can be for yourself, first. Then (and only then) can you be your best for others.

Wanna be the best mom? Wanna be the best dad? Just be the best you can be for yourself, first -- then (and only then) can you be the best parent.

Ever hear someone say, "I gave you the best years of my life?" My response to that would be: What'd you do that for? Why wouldn't you give yourself the best years of your life?

People who continue to sacrifice themselves for others never achieve their full potential, and most of the time, end up resenting who they have sacrificed for.

HERE'S THE SECRET: Don't make a sacrifice. Make a commitment to you (most important person in the world) to be your best. At all times.

How much time should **70** I invest in promoting and positioning my business?

SMART ANSWER: As much as you can.
SMARTER ANSWER: More than you think you should. While advertising gives you brand recognition, and may build awareness, it does not build value in the mind of the potential customer. And, does little or nothing for your existing customers.

Take a look at this book -- is it an ad? Well, kind of. It's valuable information about and for you, but it's also promotion about me. You're either reading this book on an airplane, or at home, or at work, or on vacation, but the bottom line is, you're reading it. It's going to help you. You're carrying it with you. Would you carry my ad? I doubt it.

Same with you and your business. Real promotion, real positioning, has to have enough value that your customer or your prospective customer will see it, or read it, or be involved in it. Enough to want more from you. Look carefully at the way I promote and position myself: articles, books, and a weekly e-mail magazine (*Sales Caffeine*) that reaches millions of salespeople. It builds my brand awareness and my perceived value to others.

I don't advertise. I position. I don't advertise. I promote. Well, that's not 100% true. I *only* advertise *after* I have positioned myself as a value provider, and *after* I've positioned myself as a consistent performer. After I have positioned myself as a leader, and a thinker, and after I have done several successful promotions (like books and seminars), then I advertise. I have name and brand recognition, and the ad works.

FINAL ANSWER:

The biggest mistake businesses make is advertising before they have become well known.

I have built my brand based on value, and now I can reinforce my brand with an ad. If you read my column every week in the paper or have bought a book of mine (like this one), and *then* you saw my advertisement for a seminar, you might spend $100 to come see me. If you didn't know me, would you spend the $100? I doubt it.

How am I helping my customers build their business?

What the hell are you asking me for? Shouldn't you pretty much know that answer?

Does your customer want to buy from you -- or make more sales? Does your customer want to buy from you -- or make more profit? Does your customer want to buy from you -- or keep their customers loyal? Does your customer want to buy from you -- or keep their employees loyal? Does your customer want to buy from you -- or have no problems?

> Once you understand
> that the customer wants
> to win for themselves,
> rather than buy from you,
> you've put your thinking
> on the right path.
> The secret is to take action.

FINAL ANSWER: Ask yourself what you can do to help your customer in the area of sales, profit, productivity, loyalty, morale, and other areas important to them. Anything you can help them with, any answers you can provide for them, any ideas you can give them, will enhance your value, and build their loyalty to you.

What am I doing to earn my customer's loyalty?

Loyalty begins after a sale has been made, and a product or service has been delivered. At this moment the customer begins to judge your value based on their perception. They begin to judge your quality based on their perception. They begin to judge your service based on their perception. And they begin to judge how they feel about you, based on their perception.

KEY WORDS: Their perception.

Their perception is your reality. Great service can be provided, but loyalty has to be earned.

It seems funny to me that many companies have promotional gimmicks they refer to using the word "loyalty." Probably the biggest of them all are airlines who provide travel miles to keep customers loyal. It has almost reached joke proportion.

Airlines aren't earning loyalty, they are simply bribing people with a free flight. And the cost of the bribe has doubled or tripled over the past year, depending upon the airline. You're not loyal to the company. You're loyal to the miles.

If the airlines did away with the miles, would you still be loyal? Answer: Not even close.

FINAL ANSWER: The easiest way to learn this loyalty lesson is to reverse it. Look at the people or the businesses that you are loyal to. Why are you loyal to them? It might be your ice cream parlor, grocery store, dry cleaner, coffee shop, car dealership, clothing store, might even be your computer repairman. Every one of them has earned your loyalty. Figure out what they do, and do that.

Loyalty is earned with friendliness, responsiveness, ease of doing business, fair value, and the good feeling customers get when they call you, visit you, or interact with you.

MY CUSTOMERS ARE
INCREDIBLY LOYAL. IT'S MY
FIRST THREE HUSBANDS
I HAD PROBLEMS WITH.

How vulnerable am I to our competition?

73

ANSWER: More than you could ever imagine. Do you have a hot list? You know, a hot prospect list? Sure you do. Do you think your competition has a hot list? Sure they do. You know who is on it? Your biggest customers.

Your competitors are plotting and planning how to take your biggest customers away from you. Right now. Think about this...have you ever taken a customer away from your competitor? Sure you have! Don't you think they want to do the same to you? You bet they do.

As a matter of fact, your competitors are meeting at this very moment on the other side of town about how to kick your ass. They are hoping that you're resting on your previous laurels. They're hoping that you don't answer the phone with a live human being. They're hoping that your Web site is inadequate. They're hoping that your sales team is poorly trained. They're hoping that they can lower their price and beat you, because of no differentiated value.

FINAL ANSWER: Your vulnerability to your competitor *never* goes away. The only problem is you're not taking it seriously enough. That is, until you lose one, and then it's too late. Why don't you just spend half of what you would have spent to win them back to try to keep them loyal?

FINAL AHA! Invest as much in your existing customers as you do in trying to attract new ones.

What do I need to learn to get ahead? What do I have to do to get ahead?

74

Want to get ahead? I'm going to give you the Realities and Strategies of Sales Success – your job is to make an implementation plan for each one.

1. Get and stay likeable. The customer buys you *first*. Sell yourself *before* you try to sell your company or your product.

2. Make a list of what you say you do that your competition does NOT say they do. There is *nothing* on the list! In other words, get creative and say something new. **HINT:** Add new questions that your competition doesn't ask.

3. Since there are NO new objections – get rid of the existing ones. Make a list of the objections you hear over and over (not interested, happy with present supplier, price too high, no budget, send me a proposal, and so many more), and figure out answers that win, and use those instead of the ones you're using.

4. Get the prospect hot for you. Make a copy of your traditional customer "hot list," then ask yourself the question "Hot for who?" Make a list of prospects that are hot to do business with you. Is it a smaller list?

5. Try it as soon as you learn it. After you listen to a strategy or sales technique, try to use it within the hour. Listening followed by doing -- leads to mastery.

6. Modify what you learn and adapt it to your personality.
Don't do it the way I do it. Do it the way that suits your personality and style. Be yourself.

7. Adapt what you learn to your product or service. Not all sales information is about what you sell. So what? Just figure out how what they teach applies to you and try that.

8. Get and keep a positive attitude by studying attitude every morning. The secret of attaining attitude is reading for 15 minutes every morning. I've been doing it for 30 years and so far it's working.

9. Join Toastmasters™. Invest an hour a week learning how to get better at presentation skills. Your presentation skills are as important as your sales skills. Go to www.toastmasters.org and find the club nearest you.

10. Stay a student – if possible, a humble student. The best way to become a master at what you do is to combine "study" with "practice" for the rest of your life.

10.5 The daily dose. You can't do it all at once -- but you can do a little each day. Everyone knows "an apple a day," but very few follow the advice. If you do nothing each day – at the end of a year that adds up to nothing. If you just do a little each day, at the end of a year it adds up to a lot. You don't get great at sales in a day – you get great at sales day by day.

FINAL ANSWER: Getting ahead is not a natural progression. Getting ahead is a result of your dedication and determination. And you are in complete control. You decide how much you want to get ahead. You decide how much you want to succeed. And you determine it with two words: Take action.

PART FIVE

Building the Friendship.
Building the Relationship.
Earning the Referral.
Earning the Testimonial.
Earning the Reorder.

*PLEASE BUY FROM ME,
I'LL BE YOUR BEST FRIEND!*

*IT WORKED IN THE
SECOND GRADE, BUT IT
DOESN'T WORK IN SALES.*

75

How easy is it to do business with me?

QUESTION: How much do you hate automated (computer) answering systems?

QUESTION: Do you use automated answering systems?

It's easy to talk about lousy service and lousy business practices when it's someone else's company, but it's much more difficult to address it in your own backyard.

When I ask my audiences if they are frustrated by or hate automated telephone systems, EVERY SINGLE PERSON RAISES A HAND -- SOMETIMES TWO HANDS. With all the grumbling about automated telephone systems, you would think someone would get it. But this is only one minor source of frustration that drives customers to competitors.

To make sure you don't drive your customers away, implement the following 6.5 steps that create customer loyalty by making it easy to do business with you:

1. Be available to sell when I need to buy. Can I place an order 24/7? Can I buy on-line, on the phone, or in-person? Anything less is not easy.

2. Have live human beings answer the phones. If a customer wants to place an order, or has a question or a problem, how easy is it to talk to a person? How easy should it be?

3. Hire friendly people. Answer this VERY IMPORTANT question: How friendly are your people?

4. Take advantage of leading-edge technology. Are you two steps ahead of your competitors? Are you using technology to save time, money, and to be more productive?

5. Identify the reasons your customers are leaving and fix them. Take action to eliminate any internal problems.

6. Identify the reasons your customers are buying and enhance them. Take action to increase selling opportunities.

6.5 Be your own customer. Would you do business with you? Call once a week to find out what it's like to do business with your company.

FINAL ANSWER: Many of you reading this are going to be frustrated because you're thinking, "There's nothing I can do about it." Well, you're wrong. Contact your five best customers. Ask them to call your company and try to place a large order five minutes before the start of your business day. Then ask them to e-mail their experience to you. Forward that e-mail to your CEO, and sit back to watch the sparks fly.

You may be corporately handcuffed, but your CEO knows that your customers fill your bank accounts, and pay his salary.

If you would like to fill your corporate bank accounts, refocus and redouble your efforts on the people that fill them first: your present customers.

How friendly are the employees at my company? How friendly is my boss? How friendly am I?

How important is friendly?
To me, if there are 100 qualities of
a successful customer service person
or salesperson, friendly is in the
top three, and may be the top one.

☺ **Friendly makes sales**. Friendly generates repeat business.

☺ **Friendly is a quality**. Like all qualities, there are varying levels of competency.

☺ **Friendly is a degree.** What's the temperature of friendly in your place of business? Is it warm or cold where you work?

And hey, if the degree of friendly in your place of business is somewhere between *medium* and *un* (friendly), here's a question that will make you squirm: *What's the relationship between friendly staff and loyal customers?*

Answer: One breeds the other.

Well, if friendly is so important, then why isn't everyone friendly? Good question. It seems so easy. One reason is that people are too serious about everything -- especially bosses, and they set the tone for the rest of the people. Is your boss friendly? Is your CEO friendly? He or she sets the tone for the company. Executive friendliness sets the tone for frontline people.

Do friendly businesses make it? Nordstrom is friendly. Ask them.

SECRET:

The corporation big wigs
(or small business owners)
need to create a friendly environment
and train people to be friendly,
and be (act) friendly all the time.
Friendly has to be "on-purpose."

And the final question is: How friendly are you? If you've become disgruntled, cynical, and in general a hot-and-cold person, it's time to renew or move on. Friendly, like attitude, is internal. It's not about your circumstances, it's about your desire to be nice to others...all the time.

FINAL ANSWER: The value of friendly is beyond measure. It costs nothing, yet it's worth a fortune. It creates a company's reputation and it creates *your* reputation. It's the most contagious disease known to man -- *catch it, and spread it.*

How can
I establish rapport?

The best way to win the sale is to first win the prospect. If you find common subjects or interests with a prospect, you can establish a business friendship. People are more likely to buy from a friend than a salesman.

What do you do to establish rapport? Do research and ask questions. Are you smart enough, sincere enough, and observant enough to find something besides business to open the conversation?

Here are some strategies you can try:

On an appointment in a prospect's office or place of business, look for clues as soon as you walk in. This is the easiest place to establish rapport. Pictures, plaques, awards on the wall, or magazines subscribed to that don't match the business. When you get in the prospect's office, look for pictures of children or events, bookcase items, books, diplomas, awards, desk items, or anything that reveals personal likes and/or after business pursuits. Ask about an award or trophy. Ask about a diploma or picture. Your prospect will be glad to talk about what he/she just did or likes to do.

Try to captivate him or her in intelligent conversation with engaging questions about their interests. It's obviously better if you're well versed in the subject, because that's where rapport is established. And if you both have avid interest, that's *common ground*, which is the secret of building rapport.

Get the prospect to talk about their passions and what makes them happy. And if it's a passion of yours -- PRESTO.

Use humor. Get the prospect to laugh. Laughing is bonding, and sets a relaxed stage for a positive presentation.

When the prospect comes to your place of business it's more difficult to establish common ground, because you don't have the advantage of the telling items that would be present in their surroundings. So, tour them around your place, and listen carefully to their remarks. They will tell you if there's something in you that sparks interest in them.

Be friendly. Ask engaging questions just below the surface. Surface questions or talk such as the weather, or did you find the place okay, should be avoided at all costs. Try to find out what they did last weekend, or what they're doing this weekend. Ask about a movie or a ballgame. Avoid politics, religion, their personal problems, and for goodness sakes don't lament your problems.

FINAL ANSWER: People love to talk about themselves. Ask the right question and it's tough to shut them up. The object is for you to find a subject, idea or situation that you *both* know about or are interested in. You're on a mission. A sales mission. But I can assure you the mission is most likely to be accomplished if you have made a friend before you make the presentation.

What is the best way to begin a relationship?

78

Your mom said it best. As a child, when you were fighting or arguing with a sibling or friend, your mom would say, "Billy, you know better than that! Now you make friends with Johnny." Your mother never told you to use the alternative of choice close or the sharp angle close on Johnny. She just said make friends. That may have been one of the most powerful sales lessons you ever got.

It is estimated that 50% of sales are made because of friendship.

I say the number is higher.

In the South it's called "the good old boys network." In the North they say it's "who you know," but it's really just friendship selling.

If you think you're going to get the sale because you have the best product, the best service, or the best price -- dream on, Bubba. You're not even half right. If 50% of sales are made on a friendly basis, and you haven't made friends with the prospect (or customer), you're missing 50% of your market.

Friends don't need to sell friends using sales techniques.
Think about it, you don't need sales techniques when you
ask a friend out, or ask for a favor - you just ask. Wanna
make more sales? You don't need more sales techniques,
you need more friends.

Think about your best customers. How did they get that
way? Don't you have great relationships with them? If you're
friends with your best customers, it will (often) eliminate
the need for price checking, price negotiating, and delivery
time demands. You can even *occasionally* screw up and still
keep them.

There's another huge bonus to being
friends -- competition is virtually
eliminated. Your fiercest competitor
couldn't blast you away from a
customer who is also a friend.

Most salespeople think that unless they are calling a
customer to sell something that it's a wasted call. Nothing
could be further from the truth.

How do you start building friendships and relationships?
Slowly. It takes time to develop a relationship. It takes time
to build a friendship. If you are reading this and thinking
"I don't have time for this relationship stuff, I'm too busy
making sales," find a new profession -- this one won't
last long.

A different venue than the office will begin building friendships and relationships. Here are a few places to meet or take your customer: a ball game, the theater, a concert, a gallery crawl, a Chamber after hours event, a community help project, a breakfast, a lunch, a dinner, a seminar given by your company. If your customer has kids, get a few tickets to the IMAX theater in your town, and go on the weekend. Talk about solidifying a relationship -- the IMAX theater is fun, and it ain't just for kids.

Having moved from the North to the South has helped me understand the value of business friends. They are much easier to establish in the South.

I'm often in conversations where someone is lamenting the fact they can't get into or around the so-called "Good old boy" network. That is the biggest bunch of baloney, and lamest sales excuse I've heard. All the salesperson is saying is that he has failed to establish a relationship or make a friend AND SOMEONE ELSE HAS.

SECRET:

You can earn a commission
using a sales technique
and making a sale.
You can earn a fortune
building friendships
and relationships.

Where should I network?

Network where your customers go. It's likely you'll find more prospects there, just like them. And, your customers are right there to be testimonials for you.

Networking in high probability environments is an answer, but not *the* answer.

Networking is a matter of choice. All I am asking you to do is make a smart one. And then show up, prepared to do business.

FINAL ANSWER: If you're looking for *the* answer, it's having a networking plan that includes about 10 hours a week. It can be a business group. It can be a trade association meeting. It can be a ball game. It can be the theatre. It can be an exercise group. It can be a gallery crawl. It can also be a charity event. I've met some of my best prospective customers running road races. At 7 a.m. before a 10k event, everyone pretty much look likes everyone else. No suits. No gatekeepers. Just people trying to beat their personal best. And, at the end of the race, people are willing to talk -- about anything.

Free Red▲Bit:

Want my list of the 15.5 best places to network? Go to www.gitomer.com, register if you are a first time user, and enter the word NETWORKING in the RedBit box.

How do I develop a powerful 30-second commercial?

Often referred to as an elevator speech, or a cocktail commercial, I named it a 30-second personal commercial because I felt you would understand it based on all the personal commercials that you've seen on television. Some of which grab your attention. Most of which make you grab the remote.

The key to a 30-second commercial is the word "engagement."

Can you engage the other person in a way that they will be interested in conversing with you? After the 30 seconds is up, you'll pretty much know whether they're engaged or not by the way they respond.

After you deliver your message, your job is to begin questioning to find something that you have in common with the other person (home town, college, kids, sports teams). If you have engaged well with your personal commercial, and you have found something in common, then it's likely you can gain an appointment, and potentially a customer.

Personally, I like to ask questions first, and give my commercial second. I like to know about the other person before I tell them about me. But I'm *very* experienced at engaging.

Here are some examples of 30-second commercials:

THE "GIVE FIRST" COMMERCIAL: A five-second question that will completely engage the other person without you ever saying one word about yourself. Exchange names, and then say the following: "Bill, I meet a lot of people, and one of the best ways for me to get to know them, and for them to know me, is to ask 'What's the perfect customer for you?' And after you're done, I'll search my mental database and see if I know anyone that might be a good prospect for you."

THE "WHAT DO YOU DO?" COMMERCIAL: This question has been asked thousands of times. Someone is *asking* for your 30-second commercial. I take my coin business card, hand it to the person and say, "I'm the best sales trainer in the world." People are forced to look at the coin. Most have never seen a coin-card. We may chat about it for a minute. Then I ask, "How many of your salespeople didn't make their sales-goal last year?" And we're off to the races. Fully engaged.

THE FUNNY COMMERCIAL: When someone asks me what I do, I say, "I help large companies with their sales training budgets, until there's none left."

THE FUNNIER COMMERCIAL: I was sitting next to my photographer, Mitchell Kearney. We were giving 30-second commercials to our networking group. Mitchell had one of my books in his hand opened to a photo of me that he had taken. Suddenly (without warning), he grabs me by the shirt, yanks me out of my chair and yells, "Ya see this guy?" Then, pointing to my photo in the book, yells, "I made him look like this!" The crowd roared, and Mitch made sales that morning. A 10-word commercial. Maybe the best one ever.

THE "CREATING A DEFICIT" COMMERCIAL: (You sell life insurance and financial plans.) Begin by asking two questions: "Bill, how much money do you think you'll need to retire?" (You wait for an exact answer.) "And how much of that do you have right now?" (And you wait for an exact answer.) And then say, "My job is to get you from where you are, to where you want to be. And I don't know if I can help you or not, but if you'll bring some of your pertinent data to a short breakfast at our mutual convenience, I'll take a look at it. If I think I can help you, I'll tell you. And if I don't think I can help you, I'll tell you that too. Is that fair enough?"

IMPORTANT NOTE: No matter what type of commercial you give, make certain that the other person knows what you do when you're done. Being vague makes everyone think you're in some form of multi-level marketing scheme. Whatever it is that you tell people, be proud of it. And be enthusiastic about it.

THE UNFAIR ADVANTAGE: If I'm going to a trade show or a networking event, I'll take a dozen books with me, and sign them to some of the people I meet. For the cost of a book, it creates a whole different level of engagement.

If there's a secret to a 30-second commercial, it is: Keep it to 30-seconds.

Free Red Bit:

If you'd like some ideas about how to ask better engagement questions, go to www.gitomer.com, register if you are a first time user, and enter the words SMART QUESTIONS in the RedBit box.

How much time should I devote to networking?

The amount of time you spend networking should be in direct proportion to the number of relationships you want to enhance, and the number of customers you want to build friendships with.

When I moved to Charlotte 18 years ago, I didn't know anyone. Well, I knew one person -- but he didn't know anyone. So, I began to network.

The first thing I did was join the Charlotte Chamber of Commerce and figure out what meetings I should attend to get to know other small business people.

The second thing I did was subscribe to the *Charlotte Business Journal,* and read it from cover to cover every week. I looked at the stories, I looked at the ads, and I especially looked at the meeting schedule in the back of the paper to see if there were any important meetings or trade shows that I should be attending.

As I began making friends, I decided I needed something that differentiated me from the others. So, I made a business card for my cat, Lito. Her title was "Corporate Mascot." My cat immediately became an icon, and everywhere I went, someone would always come up to me and ask for her business card. That was 18 years ago. People still ask.

My networking time continued to increase until eventually I was networking 20 hours a week. That included singing karaoke twice a week at an upscale bar where all the Charlotte bigwigs went. I got to meet them singing songs.

How much should you network? At least five hours a week and more like 10.

One word of caution: Results from networking don't happen in a short space of time. Your best results will come from consistently showing up and giving value.

FINAL ANSWER: If you really want to profit from the time you devote to networking and connecting -- start with my next book, *The Little Black Book of Connections*.

What are the secrets of networking success?

Many people go to networking events. Very few actually know how to network effectively. Below are some techniques and tools you can use to be a more effective, productive, and profitable networker.

The fundamental rules of networking are…

1. Show up early, ready to work, full of cards. Prepared and enthusiastic.

2. If you attend a business event with a friend or associate, split up. It's a waste of time to walk, talk, or sit together.

3. Walk the crowd once. Get familiar with the people and the room.

4. Shake firmly. No one wants to shake hands with a dead fish.

5. Make your 30-second commercial compelling to listen to. Ask and tell.

6. Have your 30-second commercial down pat. But not canned.

7. Be happy, enthusiastic, and positive. Don't be grumbling or lamenting your "tough day." People want to do business with a winner, not a whiner.

8. Don't waste time if the person isn't a good prospect. Disengage gracefully.

9. Don't butt-in. Interrupting can create a bad first impression. Stand close by, and when a pause or opening appears, jump in.

10. Eat early. It's hard to eat and mingle. Get your fill when you first arrive so you are free to shake hands, talk without spitting food, and work the crowd effectively.

11. Don't drink. If everyone else is a bit loose, you'll have the distinct advantage by being sober. Have a few beers after the event to celebrate all your contacts.

11.5 Stay until the end. The longer you stay, the more contacts you'll make.

FINAL ANSWER: If you say, "I go to networking events, but I don't get many prospects," it means you're not following the fundamentals, *or* you're not networking where your prime prospects are. Networking works. You may not be working it to your advantage.

ONE MORE THOUGHT: Event selection is as important as networking itself. Each week your Business Journal publishes a list of business events, and your Chamber publishes a monthly calendar. And don't overlook social and cultural events as networking possibilities. Select those events that may attract your customer, or people who you want to get to know.

How do I get better leads than anyone else?

The easy answer is by finding
the highest quality, most qualified prospect
who has lots of money and needs
what it is that you're selling.
If you'd like a list of these people,
they're available over there at Disney World,
in the area known as Fantasyland.

HERE'S THE REAL ANSWER:

The highest quality lead is an unsolicited referral.
(The prospect calls you directly and wants to buy.)

The second highest quality lead is a proactive referral
from a customer. (Your customer calls you and gives you the
name of someone who he thinks want to buy -- or who he
says wants to buy.)

The third highest quality lead is a reactive referral from a
customer. (One that you ask for, and the customer gives you
without a lot of prodding.)

Next is networking. Your ability to go face to face in a
group of prospective customers.

Let's say you sell roofing supplies and you're at the homebuilders' monthly meeting. All the contractors and builders, who could be your customers, are there. You have three choices:

1. You can show up, have a few beers, chit chat with everybody (including your co-workers), maybe even make an appointment, and then go home. Bad choice.

2. You can preplan the meeting by selecting the four or five people with whom you want to connect. Call them or e-mail them in advance and tell them you're looking forward to seeing them at the meeting. Good choice.

3. The best choice is to be the featured speaker at the meeting. Your topic might be -- "The roof is leaking, now what?" And give a talk that helps builders or contractors maintain their profitability and their quality. After the speech, everyone will come up and say "Great speech!" Literally, you'll meet everyone in the room. GREAT CHOICE!

FINAL ANSWER: I still recommend you select and connect with your targets. This way you can accomplish knowing everyone -- and selling a few. But the secret ingredient is being the perceived leader, so that quality people will be attracted to you.

How do I get testimonials?

Two Words: Earn them. You earn them between the time you make a sale, and when your customer needs product again. The way you serve them, the way you service them, the way you respond to them, and the way you communicate with them determines the fate of your relationship, and the fate of your reputation.

Your customers will talk about you. The only question is: how? The more on-time you are, the more friendly you are, the more valuable you are, the more memorable you are -- the more likely you are to get a proactive testimonial.

Don't confuse earning a referral with earning a testimonial. A **testimonial** is kind words spoken about you. A customer testimonial is the proof that what you have said is true, and the claims that you make are valid. A **referral** is a lead to a prospective new customer. Treating the customer right, or treating the customer beyond their expectation will earn you both. But a testimonial can make hundreds of sales for you.

FINAL ANSWER: You will only get the testimonial if you deserve it. The testimonial is a report card. It's not only proof that you performed, it's proof that the customer has faith in you (faith enough to put his name next to yours).

Earning a testimonial is all about being best or beyond. Take another peek at question 3, How do I be my best every day?

How powerful is a testimonial in completing a sale?

A testimonial is the
single surest route
to *risk-removal*
in the mind
of the prospect.

Think about your own life. You're thinking about buying a home in a new neighborhood. The street you've chosen is half-full. The salesperson keeps telling you, "When the street is full, the houses will begin to appreciate, and we anticipate at least a 30% rise in home values. The time to act is now."

You're thinking, "I love the home, *and* I can afford the home!" So you decide to go and talk to a few of your prospective neighbors. Two of them say their house is falling apart. One of them says their car was broken into. One of them says the builder never completed the repairs they promised. And one of them said they're putting their house up for sale next month.

Still want the house? Still like the house? Still want the house that the salesperson told you was going to appreciate in value?

Or do you have a different appreciation for the neighborhood now that you've talked to the neighbors? Testimonials beat salespeople, *and* your emotional decision to buy. Pretty powerful, huh?

Now lets look at the reverse. Suppose you had gone out to your prospective neighbors, and every single one of them said, "This is the greatest place we ever lived. We love our neighbors. It's completely safe. Our kids love the pool. Our homes have all gone up in value."

What's your decision now? You're going to buy that house as fast as you can.

FINAL ANSWER: The testimonial will either reinforce or destroy a salesperson's words. A testimonial can make a sale when a salesperson cannot.

> Look! Up in the sky. It's a bird!
> It's a plane! **It's a testimonial!**
> More powerful than
> a speeding salesman,
> able to leap sales objections
> in a single bound.
> And who, disguised as
> a mild-mannered third party,
> stands for truth, justice,
> and the American way (of sales).

What am I doing to prevent the loss of my best customers?

The answer is: Most likely nothing.

Most companies take their best customers for granted. So do most salespeople. Most companies brag about how much their best customers love them, but don't do anything proactively to ensure their business. So do most salespeople.

Here are 3.5 ideas to keep your best customers loyal:

IDEA 1: Schedule quarterly meetings to determine how your customer's expectations are being met. Invite BOTH buyers AND users. Open frank discussions with all levels of those who use your product or service. For example, you may sell the purchasing department your copy machines, but the office manager and the administrative staff are the ones who use them. You may have a great relationship with the purchasing agent, and think the next sale is in the bag, but the secretarial staff hates your machines, hates your service, and hates you. At this very moment they may be drafting a letter about your copiers titled: "Get these paperweights outta here." Focus your attention on all people at all levels who use your product or service.

IDEA 2: Communicate with customers weekly -- something other than a sales message. I use my e-mail magazine called Sales Caffeine. People get a weekly value message from me that has valuable sales tips, ideas, and strategies. What do your customers get?

IDEA 3: Create partnership programs where you work together for the common good. Community efforts, charities, even a golf tournament. Something that you all do "together" that builds the relationship and builds the bond.

IDEA 3.5 Create a testimonial ad campaign using your 10 best customers. Think about a full-page ad in your trade journal or local business journal, that month after month features your best customers saying why they love you, and how great you are. Then think about your competition reading the ad and realizing that their hopes of stealing your customers have been bashed. Build loyalty *and* piss off the competition. What could be better?

FINAL ANSWER: The loss of a big customer is not only financially devastating, it's emotionally devastating. It creates a loss of morale, a loss of confidence in the company, and a big black cloud hanging over the business. Invest the money in keeping customers loyal. It's insurance. Customer insurance.

REALITY CHECK: If you lose a big customer, what are you willing to spend to get them back? ANSWER: Way more than it would have cost you to invest in keeping them.

Am I available to my customers when they need me?

24.7.365
That's the minimum acceptable availability time.

Ever order anything on the Internet after 10 o'clock at night? Of course you have. Everyone has. Can you go out to the store at 11 o'clock at night? Or buy that toy at a retail store at midnight? People buy automobiles nowadays at 1 o'clock in the morning, and think nothing of it.

Do you think your customers are any different?

Customers need service all the time. And of course, customers wanna buy something all the time.

And they will buy from the source that is most available. It took big chain bookstores almost two years to realize that Amazon.com was not a joke. They have spent the last 10 years and millions of dollars trying to catch up to a competitor they thought was a mere gnat when they began. That gnat has now grown into a swarm of locusts that descends on big chain bookstores' sales like a plague.

Big chain bookstores' inability to recognize that customers would buy books at midnight cost them hundreds of millions of dollars.

Here are 5.5 things you can do to ensure that you're ready when your customer needs you:

1. Answer your phone with a live human being 24.7.365.
Yes it costs a little more, but the phrase "In order to serve you better, please select from the following seven options," is not only an annoyance to every customer that calls, it's also a bold-faced lie.

2. Make your Web site "service friendly." Can you schedule a service call on your Web site? Can you give service answers?

3. Make your Web site "question friendly." Everyone has frequently asked questions -- but it seems as though those are never the questions I want answers to. Just how helpful and interactive is your questioning capability?

4. Make your Web site "sales friendly." Can your customer place an order? Is your e-commerce user friendly? Can your customer buy in one click?

5. Create automatic or rapid response to all Internet or e-mail inquiries. People expect "instant" -- don't disappoint them.

5.5 Make yourself available before and after hours.
Give customers your cell phone number. Give customers your e-mail address.

CHALLENGE: Go to your competition's Web site, and try to buy something at midnight. Try to schedule a service call. Try to contact someone by e-mail. Now go to your own site and do the same thing. Did you win? Now call your competition on the phone. Try to place an order for $100,000. Call yourself and do the same.

The person who's easiest to do business with is the one who wins.

What value am I bringing to my customer beyond my product and service?

Before you read the answer to this, I want you to think about it. Most salespeople make a sale, deliver a product or a service, try to respond to their customer in time of need, maybe even try to build a relationship with a lunch or a ball game, and then go in and beg for the second sale. Or worse, they bid on it.

Any salesman claiming to have a relationship, and having to bid on a job, is not living in reality. Is that you? You may be friendly to customers. They may be friendly to you. But, if your price is two-cents higher, you lose. What is that? Relationships are not based on pennies. Relationships are built on value. So are re-orders.

> Value is what you do up front,
> *before* the sale, and what you
> do *during* the relationship.
> You don't add value -- You give value.

Value must be perceived by the customer. If you think it's value, and your customer sees no value, it's worthless. If I had to define "value" in a sentence it would be: "What's in it for them?"

VALUE IS: How you can help your customer use your product or service to make a profit.

VALUE IS: How you can help your customer use your product or service to produce more.

VALUE IS: About process and outcome -- not about sale.

Flying from Charlotte to Newark, I heard a guy behind me tell his boss on a cell phone "I have good news, and I have bad news. The good news is we had the best product and the best presentation among all the other competitors. The bad news is they thought our price was way out of line." That's a classic example of a salesman with no passion *and* no balls. If the prospect thought they were the best, why couldn't he get them to buy?

MAJOR CLUE: His price was not out of line. Somebody buys a Chevy. Somebody buys a Mercedes. Out of line was value. There was zero value perception from the customer's point of view. Therefore, all that was left was price.

FINAL ANSWER: I give value beyond my product or service by writing books and articles that have valuable information readers can use, by speaking at public venues or at association meetings, by communicating to my customers through my weekly e-mail magazine, by helping others without expectation, and by being outcome driven.

When people see the value, and experience the value of what I do, they buy.

Why will some customers leave?

Because they were ready to leave. Because you gave them the opportunity to leave. Because they were left unprotected, and your competition lured them away. Because they felt under-valued. Because they were under-served. Because you were too difficult to do business with. Because they had an unresolved problem, or a bunch of unresolved problems. Because your response to their needs was slow or unreliable.

NOT because they got a lower price. Lower price was the symptom; you caused them to act on the problem. Your best customers pay your price.

HERE'S THE REAL QUESTION: What are you doing to prevent more losses? Have you identified the real reasons customers leave, or are you just whining about "price?"

If you don't fix the problem, more "price excuses" will occur. More customer losses will occur.

FINAL ANSWER: List the last 10 customers you lost. Call them and ask them, "Why?" Dig deep. It may take three or four "whys" to uncover the real reason they left. Once you have the real reasons -- FIX THEM.

REPORT CARD AFTER THE FIX: Call the customers who left you, and earn their business back.

90

How do I get more referrals?

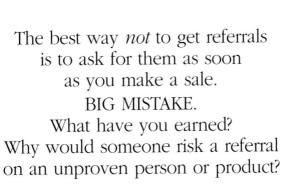

The best way *not* to get referrals
is to ask for them as soon
as you make a sale.
BIG MISTAKE.
What have you earned?
Why would someone risk a referral
on an unproven person or product?

"But Jeffrey," you whine, "my boss says I should ask for a referral as soon as I make a sale." Yeah, and your boss is dead wrong. Look, you just made a sale. How do you get the nerve to ask someone to refer you when you've delivered nothing?

You're putting your new customer in an incredibly awkward and uncomfortable position. Oh, sometimes you'll get a referral or two, but they will never whole-heartedly endorse you until you've delivered something and proven yourself.

Now that I've explained the way *you* typically ask for referrals, let me explain the *best* way to ask for referrals.

CAUTION: The method I am about to describe requires work. Most salespeople (not you of course) simply beg for referrals, rather than work for them. That's why they get so few of them.

> ## The best way to get referrals is to give them first. The second best way is to earn them.

If you combine these two, it becomes the most powerful way. And you can set that up at the end of a sale by saying the following: "Mr. Jones, I'm ecstatic that we've become your vendor of choice. After we've proven ourselves over the next few months, I'd like you to be thinking about the people that you would insist use our product or services, and let's schedule a luncheon where you might bring one or two of them to join us. And I will bring a customer or two for you."

FINAL ANSWER: Now that you know the most powerful way of getting referrals, make a list of your five best customers. Begin to think of who you know, or how you may network, to get a few prospects for each of them. That's how you start. You start by helping others. You start by giving to others. Once you begin to put giving in front of getting, your referral cup will runneth over.

What is the best way to approach and work a referral?

The best way to approach a referral is not to approach a referral.

Let the person who referred you make the first contact, and talk about you as a third-party endorsement. Maybe even set up a three-way meeting or a three-way lunch.

If somebody gives you a referral and tells you to call them, but has not called them him or herself, it's nothing more than a lead (and an awkward one at that).

A referral is the easiest sale in the world if it's set up properly. You must get your customer involved as an additional salesperson. This will remove any hesitation and any barrier.

The problem is that salespeople are so anxious to call the referral on the phone, that they do it the wrong way, and lose half their potential sales.

If you get a hundred referrals, and you engage them the right way, you should make ninety sales. If you find that the referrals are only one out of two, I assure you the fault is yours.

"Working a referral" may not be the best way to look at it. "Partnering with referrals" gives you a much clearer idea of what you need to do to maximize your percentage of sales.

The first thing you do is THANK your customer. The second thing you do is ASK FOR HELP.

STRATEGY:

1. Get your customer to give the referral as close to the sale as possible.

2. Get your customer to call and make an introduction.

3. Get your customer to set up a three-way call.

4. Get your customer to set up a three-way lunch.

4.5 Get your customer to tell you everything you need to know to make a personal impact.

FINAL ANSWER: The customer or person who gave you the referral is the *best* resource to help you make the sale. Once you have all the information you need, and the customer has set a meeting and helped you in every way possible, thank them by getting them a referral.

How many people are spreading my "word" for me?

That would depend on how powerful the word is that you're trying to spread.

Think back to Paul Revere. "The British are coming! The British are coming! One if by land. Two if by sea." That word was spread all over the countryside. And the end result was revolutionary.

If you've done something good, I mean really, really, really good, your customer will retell that story about 10 times (just like you do). If you've done something bad -- really, really bad, they'll retell the story about 50 times (just like you do).

If you've done nothing memorable either way, the odds are, no one will tell anybody anything.

Think about this:
The phone is answered
at your place of business somewhere
between 50 and 1,000 times a day.
Take the lowest number.
You have 250 opportunities per week
for someone to say something good,
nothing, or something bad.
Your choice.

Those are the easy ones. Now lets talk about the way you sell, and the way you do business. That's where the real "word" comes in.

The friendlier you are,
the easier it is to do business
with you, the more ideas
you create for others,
the more over the top
your service is, the more you
deliver beyond what you promise,
the more the "word"
will be spread about you.

FINAL ANSWER: Here's the measuring stick. If your phone is ringing with unsolicited referrals, people who said something like, "I was talking to one of your customers today, and they insisted that I call you," that means a positive word is being spread about you. If your phone is not ringing, that is also a report card, just not one you'd be proud to show your parents.

REALITY CHECK: Now that you know how powerful the answer is, what are you going to do about it? How are you going to promote yourself, how are you going to position yourself, and how are you going to sell and service in a memorable way that will create this "word?" Think of "word" as money. Because the more people spread the word, the more sales you'll make.

PART SIX

Building Your
Personal Brand

I'VE STARTED
BUILDING MY BRAND.
SO FAR, ALL I'VE GOT
IS THIS B.

BRANDO YOU'RE NOT!
I'M HUNGRY.
WHERE'S MY FOOD?

How can I differentiate myself from the competition?

All salespeople are under the false belief that because they *think* their product is better, that each customer will perceive them as different from the others. And they are wrong.

The first key differentiator is you, the salesperson. You differentiate yourself from others by the questions that you ask, the ideas that you bring into the room, and how well you communicate them.

You differentiate yourself from the others
by **BEING MORE PREPARED** than the other guy.

You differentiate yourself from the others
by **BEING MORE ENGAGING** than the other guy.

You differentiate yourself from the others
by **ASKING BETTER QUESTIONS** than the other guy.

You differentiate yourself from the others
by **HAVING A DEEPER BELIEF SYSTEM** than the other guy.

You differentiate yourself from the others
by **PROVIDING MORE PERCEIVED VALUE** than the other guy.

You differentiate yourself from the others by **THE CREATIVE IDEAS
YOU PRESENT THAT ARE BETTER** than the other guy.

You differentiate yourself from the others
by **BEING A BETTER COMMUNICATOR** than the other guy.

You differentiate yourself from the others
by **BEING MORE ENTHUSIASTIC** than the other guy.

**The reality is most products are perceived as the same.
The reality is most companies are perceived as the same.
The reality is most salespeople are perceived as the same.**

If you want to make a difference, it's the questions you ask that your competition does not ask. It's the ideas that you bring into the sales presentation that make the customer say "Wow," or at least think it.

FINAL ANSWER: The reality is there's no difference between you and the competition unless your customer or your prospect *perceives* a difference. And that perception is based 80% on the salesperson's performance and attitude.

The reality is --
the key differentiator is YOU.

I TAKE TIME TO LICK THE CUSTOMER'S FACE, I WAG MY TAIL WHEN THEY TALK, I JUMP UP AND DOWN WHEN THEY WALK THROUGH THE DOOR. THAT'S WHAT SETS ME APART FROM ALL OTHER SALES PEOPLE!

GLASBERGEN

How often am I in front of my customers?

94

ANSWER: Not often enough. Salespeople, their respective company, and *especially* their company's marketing people (or advertising agency), completely miss the mark. They think sales is all about who they are, and what they do.

Meanwhile, the customer only cares about themselves, and how they can make their business better.

"Being in front of your customer" can take place in several ways. Obviously, face-to-face meetings are the most powerful. But these meetings are always the least possible. Salespeople can't always allocate time, and customers can't always meet (or don't want to meet).

Then there are those marketing messages that you generate in a feeble attempt to "create awareness" and "build brand." Things like new literature, product bulletins, an ad campaign, and other wastes of time and money. The most consistent thing I can say about company literature and company advertising messages is that they're most often ignored or thrown away.

An ad campaign can have value *if* it employs testimonials. Otherwise, it's just a message that competes with other similar messages in the vast media wasteland.

ENTER: The "value message." A value message is something that your customer will read, benefit from, pass along to others, and look forward to the next one. A value message is something that helps your customers win, and makes you look like a winner.

REALITY CHECK: Suppose your competition was in front of your customers once a day with something of value, and all you had was literature about you and your crap? I believe you should be in front of your customers with a value message, a minimum of once per month, a maximum of once per week.

My e-mail magazine, *Sales Caffeine*, is an example of a value message. Go to www.gitomer.com and subscribe. When you get the first issue, (immediately after you sign up) you'll see what I'm talking about. It has valuable sales information that will help you sell more. And it's FREE. Get it for yourself, pass it along to others, and use it as an example to create your own.

FINAL ANSWER: Begin sending a value-based ezine to your customers at least once a month. Something short and sweet, something that defines you, something that differentiates you from the others, something that will help your customers produce more or profit more. Something they are *compelled* to send (forward) to others.

FINAL REALITY CHECK: If your company is too stupid to build and send a weekly, value-based ezine, create your own.

BIG SECRET: The single most valuable asset you (or your company) will possess over the next hundred years will be your e-mail mailing list.

What can I do to my Web site to entice my customers to buy from me?

95

E-commerce is a large portion of the future of sales. In retail it's now mandatory to be able to let customers buy online if you want to keep up with your competition. E-commerce has become a way of life, and you need to take advantage of it.

Billions are now being spent online -- but soon it will be trillions.

Almost everything can be purchased online in one form or another. Airline companies put travel agents out of business by the thousands, by simply offering their tickets for sale online.

What are you selling online?

What could you be selling online?

What should you be selling online?

Those are probably painful questions for you because your Web site's not too good, not user friendly, not sales friendly, and contains little more than your silly announcements, and your "self-talk."

Here's the test: Click on every page of your Web site and print out any page that you think is *valuable* to your customer. Not information about you or your shipping terms or your business hours -- I'm talking about things that your customer will profit from, and benefit from, in terms of them. The more value there is, the more they *may* want to buy something from you.

CHALLENGE: Click on every page of your Web site that has something to sell. Would you buy it? Have you tried to buy it? How easy is it? Have you called customers that have bought from it?

WHEW!: Take heart, your competition's Web site is probably as equally crappy as yours.

UH OH!: BUT if it isn't, you're in trouble.

FINAL ANSWER: Three key words: Make it easy. Three more key words: Make it fun. Three more key words: Make it attractive. Three more key words: Build customer value. Three more key words: Take credit cards. Three more key words: Save e-mail addresses. Three more key words: Have weekly specials. Three more key words: Do it now.

SALES BALLS: If your company's Web site sucks, make your own.

What are you "known" for?

When you were growing up, you may have had some odd talent. Making some weird noise, or doing an impression. Maybe an odd stunt, like bending your finger all the way back. Something unusual, maybe something silly, but people would come up to you and say, "Hey, do your impression of Donald Duck."

You became known for that. You probably did it so many times, you hated it. But you still did it, feeling that sense of pride that someone recognized you, and your special talent.

Fast forward to adult life, and you now have your business card printed.

Are you known for anything?
What's your special talent?
What's your special skill?

Is it still making a duck noise
or bending your finger back?
What special accomplishments have
you made that make you outstanding?
In short, what are you known for?

Are you a great writer, runner, golfer, community servant, mother, father, skier, or swimmer? Are you known at work as being the BEST? Do your customers think of you as being the best salesperson who calls on them? Are you winning awards to prove it?

Every person in sales seeks to differentiate himself or herself from the others. And the others are not just the competition. They're also your co-workers, your internal competition.

I believe that as you become known for something of value, that you will become more respected, and more readily received by those who can impact your success.

If you read question 99 about reputation, you'll see that they're similar and have similar impact. But the difference is, what you're "known for" will create differentiation, add to your reputation, and add to your acceptance.

WHAT ARE YOU
KNOWN FOR?

Are you a sales leader or a sales chaser?

Chasing your prospect too hard? People not calling you back? Pushing too hard for orders? Try running the other way -- let the prospect chase you. It's the best follow-up technique I've ever experienced.

If prospects are not returning your call, whose fault is that?

You're chasing too hard. They're running away. You couldn't get their interest. You couldn't get them to chase you.

Here are some tell-tale symptoms the chase is going the wrong way:

➤ You've followed up a few times, and now you're searching for a reason to call them -- but you can't think of one.

➤ You are uncomfortable about calling, you are unprepared, you have not established the needs of the prospect, you are unsure of their status, or you don't have much rapport with the prospect (or some of each).

➤ You call, get their voice mail, and hang up.

➤ You left your best message and they didn't call you back.

➤ They told you a decision would be made Tuesday, and Tuesday has come and gone.

➤ The prospect is giving you a bunch of lame excuses. And you are accepting them!

➤ **And the worst symptom of all** -- you are blaming the prospect for your inability to generate enough interest, create enough value, or for not having a solid reason to call you back.

Here are 3.5 ways to get them to follow you:

1. Create a sense of urgency by telling a compelling story.
A story about achievement lost because of delay. Hint at a solution. Let them think about it.

2. Give just a little information (one potato chip) about how they benefit.
Things the prospect can put into his or her life or business that they are currently without. Ask them to take some action to get the reward or answer.

3. Give information about their "Why," or what you believe to be their hottest reason for purchasing.
Everyone has a "main reason" they want to buy. It's called a "buying motive." Offer a valuable solution. Something better than they have now. Maybe even something that makes them slightly uncomfortable about their present situation -- that makes you look like a blessing -- or at least a viable alternative.

3.5 Think "profit" and "productivity" not "price" and "sale."
Your customers want to know how they'll profit from doing business with you. They want to know the value of doing business with you. They want to be assured that they gain and earn more than they want to "save money."

FINAL NOTE: It never ceases to amaze me that salespeople have no concept of what it really takes to get the customer to buy. They continue to think they have to "push" to make the sale, and nothing could be further from the truth. Persistent, yes. Pushy, no.

If chasing prospects too hard makes them run away, why are you continuing to do it? Your challenge is to lead your prospects so they will follow you -- and turn into customers.

What am I recognized as being the "THE BEST" at?

This may be the most important answer in the book.

Being **BEST** is not just to make more sales. It's to advance your life and yourself. Early in my career, a fellow speaker named Bert Dubin taught me about experts. He said there were three kinds of experts: an expert, a world-class expert, and THE world-class expert.

That was February, 1994. Since then, I've been on a mission. Or should I say THE mission.

How you become recognized by others will determine not only how they treat you, but also how they are willing to interact with you, build relationships with you, buy from you, be loyal to you, refer others to you, give testimonials for you, and compensate you. If your customers do not consider you **BEST**, then they will try their best to lower your price, or simply buy from someone else.

I have become "the **BEST** at what I do" by reading, thinking, observing, speaking, and writing. I don't just write about sales. I make sales, and then I write about the process.

Most salespeople are focused on monthly quotas, annual revenues, maybe getting a raise, maybe making the presidents club. All of those are okay goals. But none of them have the word **BEST** at their core. Are you the number one salesperson in your company? If you're not, "How come?" Or an even harder question, "What are you doing about it?"

And by the way, **BEST** does not only apply to your job or your profession. **BEST** also applies to dad or mom, friend or spouse.

If you're doing your **BEST**, eventually you'll become **BEST**. You may not see your own growth, because you're too close to it. But take a moment and look back over the last few years. Have you grown? Have you gotten better?

The answer is probably yes. But the question is, to what degree? Could you have done more? Did you only do what you had to do to get by?

Here's an easier way to ask that question: Which did you spend more time at: reading, or watching television? I doubt that you'll ever win the award of Best Damn Television Watcher in the U.S. (even though you may be qualified).

The only reason **BEST** is elusive is that at it's core is hard work.

BEST NOTE: As you read this, if you're doing the "dance of justification," (telling yourself how great you are, or could have been better if it wasn't for…) you're only denying yourself your own opportunity in moving from satisfaction, to success, to fulfillment. The satisfied ones always make their quota. The good ones are always successful. The **BEST** are always fulfilled.

What do the leaders in my industry say about me?

In sales, there are many different forms of a report card: the number of sales you make, the number of referrals you get, making the president's club, eliminating your car payment, beating your competition on a big deal. **To me, the most powerful report card is your personal reputation.**

When industry leaders talk, does your name come up? Do they know you exist? And if they do know you exist, what do they say about you?

Reputation is tied to success. Suppose instead of industry leaders I said, "community leaders." What do they think of you? Do they know that you exist. And if they do know that you exist, what are they saying about you?

Your reputation will most often precede you when you walk into a sale. If you have a great reputation, and are well known and respected, both for what you do and for who you are, then your position in a sales meeting will be much more powerful than if you're just doing a product pitch trying to explain (justify) to the prospect who you are.

FINAL ANSWER: Industry leaders are industry purchasers, and if they're talking about you in a good way -- that means they like you and they respect you (and without three bids -- they'll buy from you).

PART SIX POINT FIVE

The Final AHA!

I'VE GOT ALL
THE ANSWERS.
I'M READY TO GO!

YEAH, EXCEPT ONE:
WHERE'S MY FOOD?

How much do I love what I do?

Do I love sales?
Do I love what I do?
Do I love my product?
Do I love my company?
Do I love my customers?

These are not questions I pulled out of the air. These are questions that directly affect your productivity, your attitude, your income, your success, and your fulfillment -- not to mention your longevity at your present job.

Many salespeople are reluctant to come to grips with "why" they're in their present job, and why they're in sales. Some salespeople will respond, "I'm in it for the money," some will respond, "I need the money," others will respond, "I have bills to pay and debt to overcome," and even more will say, "I have a family." What you won't hear is: "I haven't saved enough to do what I really want to do." And, unfortunately, even less are willing to make a move.

If you don't love what you do, you're doing no one a favor by staying in your present position. Your attitude and morale will be negative, you'll be complaining about everything, and you'll be blaming everyone else and their dog for your unhappiness and inadequacy.

AND THERE'S A BONUS: Your boss will be all over you to increase your numbers. Your customers will be upset about your lack of attention, and you will rise to a level of mediocrity.

What are you thinking?

Some salespeople hate their job, but stay because they "make a lot of money." **CLUE:** The worst reason to keep a job is because you're making a lot of money. When money is your motive, it's all about making the sale without regard to building the relationship -- a formula for long-term disaster.

Oh, you may have some short-term success, but when you're home at night, you'll be drowning your misery in television, beer, and everything but preparation for the next day.

You can get away with this behavior for a short time, but in the end, you'll be looking in the "Help Wanted" section of the Sunday paper or posting your resume online, hoping for a better opportunity.

It's most interesting to me that the salespeople looking for a "better opportunity" are the very ones *not* looking in their own backyard. (See Russell Conwell's *Acres of Diamonds* for the full lesson.) Most salespeople fail to realize that when they become the best they can be, they will attract the right offers rather than seek them.

Let me flip back to the positive side. The purpose of this answer is to give you a formula that you can use to figure out if you're in the right place or how to find the right place.

HERE'S THE FORMULA: If you're in sales and you love sales, first ask yourself, "If I could sell anything, what would I sell?" If the answer to that question is not what you're currently selling -- you have uncovered part of the problem. However, this formula is not about switching jobs immediately, this formula is about becoming the best salesperson you can be in each job you commit to. If you're going to leave a job for another job, why don't you set the company record for most sales before you walk out the door?

Selling is a lot like running a road race. You don't have to win the race, but you do have to achieve your personal best each time you run one.

If your numbers are low or mediocre at one place, what makes you think they will be better someplace else? You see, the formula involves more than simply loving what you do -- it's also about possessing the skills to do what you love (or dedicating yourself to getting them).

Once you've determined what you love to do and have dedicated yourself to getting the skills, the third part is about believing. You must believe in your company -- believe in your product -- believe in your service -- and believe in yourself. If you believe deeply that everything is "best," your message will be so enthusiastically delivered that others will catch your passion. A deep self-belief will create enthusiasm, and a deep self-belief will create passion.

The final part is about your attitude. Attitude starts from within. It's the mood you're in when you wake up in the morning, the mood you stay in all day long, and the mood you're in when you go to bed.

But attitude is not a feeling. Attitude is a life-long dedication
to the study of positive thought and the character/charisma
that you display as you interact with others. If it's not
internal, it can never be external.

Now you have the formula. And no, I'm not going to
summarize it. If you want it, you'll read this answer again
and again.

John Patterson, the founder of the National Cash Register
Company, the father of American salesmanship, and the
subject of my book, *The Patterson Principles of Selling*,
said it best when he said, "Put your heart into your work."

Patterson loved cash registers. He couldn't understand why
everyone didn't love cash registers. Personally, I like cash
registers because most of them have cash inside. But you
may not like cash registers. You can never put your heart
into something you don't love. And so I've taken the liberty
of paraphrasing Patterson by saying, "Love it or leave it."

Here's the best news:
If you love it,
it will be ever so easy
for you to put
your full heart into it.

Jeffrey Gitomer
Chief Executive Salesman

Author. Jeffrey Gitomer is the author of The New York Times Best Seller *The Sales Bible, Customer Satisfaction is Worthless -- Customer Loyalty is Priceless, The Patterson Principles of Selling*, and his latest best-selling book *The Little Red Book of Selling*. Jeffrey's books have sold more than 800,000 copies worldwide.

Over 100 presentations a year. Jeffrey gives seminars, runs annual sales meetings, and conducts training programs on selling and customer loyalty. He has presented an average of 120 seminars a year for the past ten years.

Big Corporate Customers. Jeffrey's customers include Coca-Cola, DR Horton, Caterpillar, BMW, BNC Mortgage, Inc., Cingular Wireless, Ferguson Enterprises Inc., Hilton, Kimpton Hotels, Enterprise Rent-A-Car, Ameripride, NCR, Stewart Title, Comcast Cable, Time Warner Cable, Ingram Micro, Wells Fargo Bank, Baptist Health Care, Blue Cross Blue Shield, Carlsburg Beer, Wausau Insurance, Northwestern Mutual, MetLife, Sports Authority, GlaxoSmithKline, A.C. Nielsen, IBM, New York Post, and hundreds of others.

In front of millions of readers every week. His syndicated column *Sales Moves* appears in more than 95 business newspapers worldwide, and is read by more than 4 million people every week.

Selling Power Live. Jeffrey Gitomer is the host and commentator of *Selling Power Live*, a monthly, subscription-based sales resource bringing together the insights of the world's foremost authorities on selling and personal development.

On the Internet. His three WOW Web sites -- *www.gitomer.com*, *www.trainone.com*, and *www.knowsuccess.com* get as many as 10,000 hits a day from readers and seminar attendees. His state of the art Web presence and e-commerce ability has set the standard among peers, and has won huge praise and acceptance from customers.

Up Your Sales Online Sales Training. Online sales training lessons are available at *www.trainone.com*. The content is pure Jeffrey -- fun, pragmatic, real world, and immediately implementable. TrainOne's innovation is leading the way in the field of customized e-learning.

Sales Caffeine. Jeffrey's weekly ezine called, Sales Caffeine, is a sales wake-up call delivered every Tuesday morning to more than 100,000 subscribers free of charge. This allows him to communicate valuable sales information, strategies, and answers to sales professionals on a timely basis.

Sales Assessment Online. The world's first customized sales assessment. Renamed a "successment," this amazing sales tool will not only judge your selling skill level in twelve critical areas of sales knowledge, it will give you a diagnostic report that includes 50 mini sales lessons as it rates your sales abilities, and explains your customized opportunities for sales knowledge growth. Aptly named KnowSuccess, the company's mission is: *You can't know success until you know yourself.*

Award for Presentation Excellence. In 1997, Jeffrey was awarded the designation of Certified Speaking Professional (CSP) by the National Speakers Association. The CSP award has been given less than 500 times in the past 25 years and is the association's highest earned award.

BuyGitomer, Inc.
310 Arlington Avenue • Loft 329
Charlotte, N.C. 28203
704.333.1112
www.gitomer.com • jeffrey@gitomer.com

Thank You, Thank You!

Three years ago, on a trip to Trinidad, my client provided me with Rupert (one of his employees) as a tour guide. Every time I made a positive comment or complimented him, he would respond with a double "Thank You." It was very pleasing, and different. It was like a thank you on top of a thank you.

There are several people to whom I would like to say "Thank You, Thank You!"

To **Ray Bard** for the original idea that he brought to me for *The Little Red Book of Selling*. Ray and the entire National Book Network helped create first year sales of more than 250,000 copies, and paved the way for the book you've just read. And there will be more. **Thank You, Thank You!**

To **Jim Schachterle** for placing the initial call to me and persisting until he proved that there was a difference between all the other publishers I talked to — and Prentice Hall. **Thank You, Thank You!**

To **Tim Moore** for reinforcing everything that Jim said and creating a true partnership between publisher and writer. And for his deep rooted belief that this book will be a winner. **Thank You, Thank You!**

To **Rachel Russotto** and **Jessica McDougall** for tireless, dedicated, insightful and creative editing. For organization, for help, for loyalty, and for putting their hearts into my work. **Thank You, Thank You!**

To my brother **Josh** for his design brilliance, and for his design guidance, not to be confused with, but certainly capable of divine guidance. Our renaissance has created a formidable team that will last as long as we do. **Thank You, Thank You!**

To **Greg Russell** for incredible inside layout design and a strong desire to do his best, rather than simply lay out a book. **Thank You, Thank You!**

To my staff at Buy Gitomer and TrainOne. **Thank You, Thank You!**

To my friends, my family, and my family of customers. **Thank You, Thank You!**

"Great salespeople are not born or made. They evolve over time based on their dedication to excellence, and their willingness to serve."

-- Jeffrey Gitomer

Turn the RED into GREEN

The Little Red Book of Sales Answers
is available as a blended learning solution.
This will enable you and your organization
to take these 99.5 sales answers
and make them come alive
in your company.

The Little Red Book of Sales Answers
packaged training contains facilitator guides,
participant workbooks, multi-media support,
job aids, and e-learning reinforcement.

Call 704-333-1112 and scream,
"More Answers!"

Other Titles by Jeffrey Gitomer

The Little Red Book of Selling
(Bard Press, 2004)

Customer Satisfaction Is Worthless, Customer Loyalty Is Priceless
(Bard Press, 1998)

The Sales Bible
(Wiley & Sons, 2003)

The Patterson Principles of Selling
(Wiley & Sons, 2004)